Japan Tourism

Travel Guide, Vacation, Holiday, Business, Environmental Study

Author
Nick John

Copyright Notice

Copyright © 2017 Global Print Digital
All Rights Reserved

Digital Management Copyright Notice. This Title is not in public domain, it is copyrighted to the original author, and being published by **Global Print Digital**. No other means of reproducing this title is accepted, and none of its content is editable, neither right to commercialize it is accepted, except with the consent of the author or authorized distributor. You must purchase this Title from a vendor who's right is given to sell it, other sources of purchase are not accepted, and accountable for an action against. We are happy that you understood, and being guided by these terms as you proceed. Thank you

First Printing: 2017.

ISBN: 978-1-912483-46-4

Publisher: Global Print Digital.
Arlington Row, Bibury, Cirencester GL7 5ND
Gloucester
United Kingdom.
Website: www.homeworkoffer.com
.

Table of Content

Introduction 1
Japan in Profundity 5
  As of Today 5
  Japanese 9
    Meeting the Japanese People 10
    Etiquette 15
  Cultural Briefing 23
    Sumo 27
    Tea Ceremony 29
    Floral & Landscape Arts 31
  Food & Drink 33
    Japanese Cuisine 33
    Drinks 48
  History 49
    Ancient History (ca. 30,000 B.C.-A.D. 710) 49
    The Nara Period (710-84) 51
    The Heian Period (794-1192) 52
    The Kamakura Period (1192-1333) 53
    The Muromachi & Azuchi-Momoyama Periods (1336-1603) 54
    The Edo Period (1603-1867) 55
    Meiji Period Through World War II (1868-1945) 59
    Modern Japan (1946-Present) 61
  Language 68
  Books, Films & Music 73
  Religion 84
Travel and Tourism 87
  Planning a Trip to Japan 87
    Health & Insurance 89
    Money 92
    Actualities 97
    Visitor Information 110
    Entry Requirements & Customs 112
      Passports 112
      Entry Requirements 115
      Customs 115
      Medical Requirements 116
  Hotels 117
    Japanese-Style Accommodations 122

- Western-Style Accommodations 133
- When to Go 141
- Getting There 147
- Getting Around 148
  - By Train 149
  - By Plane 163
  - By Bus 166
  - By Car 168
  - By Ferry 170
- Advices on Dining 171
- Information for Families 180
- Escorted & Package Tours 182
- Gay and Lesbian Travelers 186
- Student Travelers 186
- Travelers with Disabilities 187
- Regions in Brief 189
  - Honshu 191
  - Hokkaido 194
  - Shikoku 195
  - Kyushu 195
  - Okinawa 196
- Historical Towns 197
  - Kurashiki Bikan Historical Quarter 197
  - Hachiman-bori 198
  - Nagasaki Shinchi Chinatown 199
  - Tensha-en Garden 200
  - Mimitsu area 202
  - Harimaya-bashi Bridge 204
  - Area of traditional warehouses 204
  - Nagamachi Buke Yashiki District 205
  - Hanamaki Area 208
  - Imabari/Ozu Area 209
  - Yuya/Asuke Area 211
  - Sanshu Asuke Yashiki 213
  - Arita 214
  - Arita/Imari Area 215
  - Tono-machi 216
  - Tsuwano Area 217
  - Rosan-do 219
  - Yamaguchi 220
  - Youkaichi Gokoku Streetscape Preservation Center 221

 Uchiko 223
 Sanno-machi Historic District 224
 Takayama Area 225
 Historic Battlefield of Nagakute 227
 Seto/Nagakute Area 228
 Hita Area 229
 Kunisaki-hanto Peninsula Area 230
 Izumi-fumoto Samurai Residences 231
 Izumi Area 233
Museum 234
 Ohara Museum of Art 234
 Bizen Pottery Traditional and Contemporary Art Museum 235
 Sea Turtle Museum "Caretta" 236
 Oita Prefectural Art Museum (OPAM) 237
 Otsuka Museum of Art 238
 Okayama-shiritsu Orient Bijutsukan 240
 Okayama Kenritsu Bijutsukan (Art Museum) 241
 Hyuga City History and Folk Museum 242
 Hokkaido Museum of Modern Art 243
 Migishi Kotaro Museum of Art 244
 Tokyo National Museum 245
 Kyoto National Museum 246
Calendar of Events 248
The Best among All 265
 My favourite Experiences 265
 The Best Museums 269
 The Best National Parks 272
 Best Dining Bets 275
 The Best Outdoor Pursuits 277
 The Best Temples & Shrines 279
 Best Hotel Bets 282
 The Best of Modern Japan 289
 The Best Castles, Palaces & Historic Homes 290
 The Best Destinations for Serious Shoppers 293
 The Best of Old Japan 295
 The Best Gardens 298

Introduction

Japan is an island country consisting of four major and numerous smaller islands. The islands lie in an arc across the Pacific coast of northeastern Asia, forming a part of the volcanic "Rim of Fire." From north to south this chain of islands measures more than 1,500 miles, but it is only about 130 miles across; its total landmass is just under 150 thousand square miles. If placed alongside the Pacific coast of North America, the Japanese islands would extend from northern Washington State to the southern tip of Baja California in Mexico, and as a result Japan has a wide variation in climate.

Japan's closest neighbors are Russia, Korea and China. In early history the Korean Peninsula acted as a bridge between Japan and the vast expanse of China, where a great civilization emerged—later on, Japan made connections with China directly by sea. As an island people, the Japanese have been aware of their physical isolation since ancient times, and this isolation has had many positive aspects. For much of

Japan's history, the seas protected it from invasion. The Japanese also controlled international contact by expanding, narrowing, and sometimes terminating diplomatic relations with other nations.

Despite such concern with managing contact with the outside world, many Japanese have admired, been curious about, and studied aspects of foreign cultures whenever they have reached their home shores. During closed periods, they digested foreign influences and, based on their tastes and necessities, transformed those influences into distinctly Japanese forms and styles.

Hardly a day goes by that you don't hear something about Japan, whether the subject is trade, travel, cuisine, the arts, or Japanese imports ranging from Sony and Toyota to karaoke and anime. Yet Japan remains something of an enigma to people in the Western world. What best describes this Asian nation? Is it the giant producer of cars and an entire array of sleek electronic goods that compete favorably with the best in the West? Or is it still the land of geisha and bonsai, the punctilious tea ceremony, and the delicate art of flower arrangement? Has it become, in its outlook and popular culture, a country more Western than Asian? Or has it retained its unique ancient traditions while forging a central place in the contemporary post-industrialized world?

In fact, Japan is an intricate blend of East and West. Its cities may look Westernized often disappointingly so but, beyond first impressions, there's very little about this Asian nation that could lull you into thinking you're in the West. Yet Japan also differs greatly from its Asian neighbors. Although it borrowed much from China in its early development, including Buddhism and its writing system, the island nation remained steadfastly isolated from the rest of the world throughout much of its history, usually deliberately so. Until World War II, it had never been successfully invaded; and for more than 200 years, while the West was stirring with the awakenings of democracy and industrialism, Japan completely closed its doors to the outside world and remained a tightly structured feudalistic society with almost no outside influence.

It's been only some 140 years since Japanese opened their doors, embracing Western products wholeheartedly, yet at the same time altering them and making them unquestionably their own. Thus, that modern high-rise may look Western, but it may contain a rustic-looking restaurant with open charcoal grills, corporate offices, a pachinko parlor, a high-tech bar with views of Mount Fuji, a McDonald's, an acupuncture clinic, a computer showroom, and a rooftop shrine. Your pizza may come with octopus, beer gardens are likely to be fitted with Astroturf, and "parsley" refers to unmarried women older than 25 (because parsley is what's left on a plate). City police patrol on bicycles; garbage collectors attack their job with the vigor of a well-trained army; and white-gloved elevator operators, working in some of the world's swankiest department stores, bow and thank you as you exit.

Because of this unique synthesis of East and West into a culture that is distinctly Japanese, Japan is not easy for Westerners to comprehend. Discovering it is like peeling an onion you uncover one layer only to discover more layers underneath. Thus, no matter how long you stay in Japan, you never stop learning something new about it and to me that constant discovery is one of the most fascinating aspects of being here

Japan in Profundity
As of Today

I'll splurge every couple of years for that perfect Issey Miyake outfit (it travels so well!), but all my friends know I'm a cheapskate at heart. That's why I consider the economic recession that hit Japan in 1992 while bad news for those who lost their jobs, including many politicians the beginning of a new Japan for frugal travelers. In contrast to the heady days of the 1980s bubble economy, when only designer goods would do and expense accounts seemed unlimited, today's Japan is a bargain-hunter's delight. Thanks to recession fallout, we have 100 Yen stores, shops selling used designer wear, buffets virtually everywhere, inexpensive set lunches in even the toniest of restaurants, and virtually every prefecture trying to figure out how to lure more international travelers. There are deals across the country only for foreigners, including regional rail passes and plane tickets. For the cheapskate, there's never been a better time to visit Japan than now.

Not that I'm heartless about the challenges facing the Japan of today. Despite the ushering in of a new government in 2009 that promises to cut government waste, boost disposable household income, and reverse almost 20 years of deflation, Japan faces mind-boggling financial, social, and political obstacles. Certainly one of Japan's biggest concerns is its declining birthrate coupled with one of the most rapidly aging populations in the world. About 22% of its population is 65 and older; by 2055, that number is expected to double. Meanwhile, Japan's ratio of children aged 14 and younger is believed to the lowest in the world, accounting for only 13.5% of the population. This will undoubtedly lead to a shortage of labor, severely straining the country's resources for tax revenues, pensions, and healthcare.

Meanwhile, bankruptcies and corporate mergers have forever altered the relationship between Japanese workers and their employers, with lifelong employment with the same company no longer a given. Homelessness is now so common that it no longer draws stares, even in the swank Ginza District. Crime, once almost unheard of, is on the rise, especially theft. My former Tokyo landlady fears burglary so much that she refuses to open her doors to strangers.

On the other hand, crime, though undeniably on the increase, is still negligible when compared to levels in the United States, and Japan remains one of the safest countries in the world. Although it's true I'm more careful than I used to be I guard my purse in crowded subways, I avoid parks after dark for Americans such precautions seem merely self-evident. But while I'm vigilant about theft and purse snatching, I never worry about personal safety. Violent crime especially against strangers remains virtually unheard of in Japan.

In any case, the attributes that drew me to Japan in the first place and keep me coming back remain strongly in place: the country's unexpected physical beauty, its safety, and its unique cuisine, customs, and culture. Japan is much the same as when I first came here, humming with energy, crowded beyond belief in its major cities, and filled with acts of human kindness. But I also like the ways Japan has changed. I like that a greater influx of foreign visitors, coupled with a young generation of less inhibited Japanese, has forever altered the social landscape. Japan is more accessible than it has ever been, and in many ways it's also more fun. Whereas in the 1980s Japan was best known as an economic powerhouse, today it's known also for its cool pop culture, from *anime* and *manga* to fashion and food. It's still the land of the geisha, but it's also the land of Hello Kitty.

The Magical World of Vending Machines

One of the things that usually surprises visitors to Japan is the number of vending machines in the country, estimated to be more than 5.5 million one for every 20 people. They're virtually everywhere in train stations, in front of shops, on the back streets of residential neighborhoods. Most will take bills and give back change. Many have almost nonsensical English-language promotional lines on them, such as ENJOY REFRESHING TIME. Some will even talk to you.

And what can you buy in these vending machines? First, there are the obvious items drinks and snacks, including hot or cold coffee in a can. But if you're on your way to someone's house, you might be able to pick up a bouquet of flowers from a machine. Your camera is out of batteries? You may be able to find those, too. Vending machines outside post offices sell stamps and postcards, while those in business hotels sell razors, cup noodles, beer, and even underwear.

In the not-too-distant past, things were also sold from sidewalk vending machines that would have met with instant protest in other countries around the world. Cigarettes and beer were available on almost every corner, where even children could buy them if they wanted to; nowadays, however, shoppers must first insert a computer-readable card certifying they're at least 20 years old. I remember a vending machine in my Tokyo neighborhood: By day, it was blank, with no sign as to what was inside; at night, however, the thing would light up, and on display were pornographic comics. Nowadays, pornographic vending machines are very rare, not for moral reasons, but because of the Internet.

Still, if it's available in Japan, it's probably in a vending machine somewhere.

Japanese

As an island nation with few natural resources, Japan's 127 million people are its greatest asset. Hardworking, honest, and proud about performing every task well no matter how insignificant it may seem, Japanese are well known for their politeness and helpfulness to strangers. Indeed, hardly anyone returns from a trip to Japan without stories of extraordinary kindnesses extended by Japanese.

With almost 99% of its population consisting of ethnic Japanese, Japan is one of the most homogeneous nations in the world. That coupled with Japan's actual physical isolation as an island nation has more than anything else led to a feeling among Japanese that they belong to a single huge tribe different from any other people on earth, and that all people can basically be divided into two categories: Japanese and non-

Japanese. You'll often hear a Japanese preface a statement or opinion with the words "We Japanese," implying that all Japanese think alike.

While in the West the attainment of "happiness" is the elusive goal for a full and rewarding life, in Japan, it's satisfactory performance of duty. From the time they are born, Japanese are instilled with a sense of duty that extends toward parents, spouses, bosses, co-workers, neighbors, and society as a whole. In a nation as crowded as Japan, consideration of others is essential, and consideration of the group always wins out over the desire of the individual. In fact, I have had Japanese tell me they consider individuality synonymous with selfishness and a complete disregard for the feelings of others.

Meeting the Japanese People

On a personal level, Japanese are among the most likable people in the world. They are kind, thoughtful, and adept in perceiving another person's needs. Japanese have an unerring eye for pure beauty, whether it be food, architecture, or landscaped gardens; it's impossible to visit Japan and not have some of the Japanese appreciation of beauty rub off.

If you're invited to Japan by an organization or business, you'll receive the royal treatment and will most likely be wined and dined so wonderfully and thoroughly that you'll never want to leave. If you go to Japan on your own as an ordinary tourist, however, chances are that your experiences will be much different. Except for those who have lived or traveled abroad, few Japanese have had much contact with foreigners. In fact, even in Tokyo, there are some Japanese who have never spoken to a foreigner and would be quite embarrassed and uncomfortable if confronted with the possibility. And even though most of them have studied English, few Japanese have had the opportunity to use the language and cannot (or are too shy to) communicate in it. So don't be surprised if you find the empty seat beside you on the subway the last one to be occupied most Japanese are deathly afraid you'll ask them a question they won't understand.

In many respects, therefore, it's much harder to meet the locals in Japan than in many other countries. Japanese are simply much shyer than Americans. Although they will sometimes approach you to ask whether they might practice English with you, for the most part you're left pretty much on your own unless you make the first move.

Probably the easiest way to meet Japanese is to go where they play namely, the country's countless bars, including those that serve *yakitori* (skewered chicken). Usually small affairs, each with perhaps just a counter and some tables, they're often filled with both younger and older Japanese, many of whom are regulars. As the evening wears on, you'll encounter Japanese who do want to speak to you if they understand English, and other slightly inebriated Japanese who will speak to you even if they don't. If you're open to them, such chance encounters may prove to be the highlight of your trip or, at the very least, an evening of just plain fun.

My co-worker Janie, who traveled around Japan with her then-3-year-old daughter, found that traveling with children opened up opportunities like a magic key. Other children talked freely to her child (they never seemed to have a language barrier), while Janie was able to talk to parents about their children. Complete strangers she met on a train even invited her and her daughter home; in contrast, some Japanese people she has known for years have never invited her home, preferring instead to meet at coffee shops or restaurants.

Another good way to meet Japanese people is to stay in a *minshuku*, an inexpensive lodging in a private home. Also, national newspapers and local English-language newsletters list international club activities; you may be able to hook up with, say, a hiking or skiing group composed of both Japanese and international members.

Finally, you can meet locals and learn about destinations at the same time through Goodwill Guides, a national organization of volunteers (mostly retirees, housewives, and students) who donate their time to guide you around their city free of charge (you pay their travel expenses, admission fees to sights, and meals). There are Goodwill Guides in cities throughout Japan, including Fukuoka, Kumamoto, Beppu, Kagoshima, Takamatsu, Matsuyama, Hiroshima, Himeji, Kurashiki, Matsue, Kobe, Osaka, Kyoto, Nara, Kanazawa, Matsumoto, Nagoya, Tokyo, Yokohama, Kamakura, Hakone, Nikko, and Matsushima. Reservations for a guide must be made in advance usually a week or more. For information, including contact information, ask for the pamphlet "Goodwill Guide Groups of Japan Welcome You," at Tourist Information Centers in Tokyo or Narita and Kansai international airports; or go to JNTO's website at www.jnto.go.jp, and click "Essential Info" (under "Arrange Your Travel"), and then "Guide Services."

The Home-Visit System Recognizing the difficulty foreigners may face in meeting Japanese people, a half-dozen or so cities offer a Home Visit, allowing overseas visitors the chance to visit an English-speaking Japanese family in their home for a few hours. Not only does such an encounter bring you in direct contact with Japanese, it also offers a glimpse into their lifestyle. You can even request that a family member share your occupation, though such requests are, of course, sometimes impossible to fulfill.

The program doesn't cost anything, but it does take some preparation. You must make arrangements in advance, which differs from city to city and can range from 1 day in advance to 2 weeks in advance, by calling or applying in person at the local administrative authority or private organization (which is sometimes the local tourist office) that handles the city's home-visit program. After contacting a local family, the office will inform you of the family and the time to visit. Most visits take place for a few hours in the evening (dinner is not served). You should bring a small gift such as flowers, fruit, or a small souvenir from your hometown.

Before your visit, you may be asked to appear in person at the application office to obtain detailed directions; or the office may call with the directions. Note that application offices may be closed on weekends and holidays. Here are a few contact numbers for cities participating in the Home-Visit System: Narita (tel. 0476/24-3232 or 24-3198; you can also apply in person at the Tourist Information Center in Terminal 2 at Narita airport), Nagoya (tel. 052/581-5689), Kyoto (tel. 075/752-3511), Osaka (tel. 06/6345-2189), Kobe (tel. 078/303-1010), Kurashiki (tel. 086/475-0543), Hiroshima (tel. 082/247-9715), Fukuoka (tel. 092/733-2220), and Kumamoto (tel. 096/359-2121). For information, contact local tourist information offices.

Etiquette

Much of Japan's system of etiquette and manners stems from its feudal days, when the social hierarchy dictated how a person spoke, sat, bowed, ate, walked, and lived. Failure to comply with the rules would bring severe punishment, even death. Many Japanese have literally lost their heads for committing social blunders.

Of course, nowadays it's quite different, although Japanese still attach much importance to proper behavior. As a foreigner, however, you can get away with a lot. After all, you're just a "barbarian" and, as such, can be forgiven for not knowing the rules. There are two cardinal sins, however, you should never commit: One is you should never wear your shoes into a Japanese home, traditional inn, temple, or any room with *tatami*; the other is that you should never wash with soap inside a communal Japanese bathtub. Except for these two horrors, you will probably be forgiven any other social blunders (such as standing with your arms folded or your hands in your pockets).

As a sensitive traveler, however, you should try to familiarize yourself with the basics of Japanese social etiquette. Japanese are very appreciative of foreigners who take the time to learn about their country and are quite patient in helping you. Remember, if you do commit a faux pas, apologize profusely and smile.

Most forms of behavior and etiquette in Japan developed to allow relationships to be as frictionless as possible a pretty good idea in a country as crowded as Japan. Japanese don't like confrontations, and fights are extremely rare. Japanese are very good at covering almost all unpleasantness with a smile. Foreigners find the smile hard to read; a smiling Japanese face can mean happiness, sadness, embarrassment, or even anger.

My first lesson in such physiognomic inscrutability happened on a subway in Tokyo, where I saw a middle-aged Japanese woman who was about to board the subway brutally knocked out of the way by a Japanese man rushing off the train. She almost lost her balance, but she gave a little laugh, smiled, and got on the train. A few minutes later, as the train was speeding through a tunnel, I stole a look at her and was able to read her true feelings on her face. Lost in her thoughts, she knitted her brow in consternation and looked most upset and unhappy. The smile had been a put-on.

Another aspect of Japanese behavior that sometimes causes difficulty for foreigners, especially in business negotiations, is the reluctance of Japanese to say no when they mean no. Many consider such directness poor manners. As a result, they're much more apt to say your request is very difficult, or they'll simply beat around the bush without giving a definite answer. At this point, you're expected to let the subject drop. Showing impatience, anger, or aggressiveness rarely gets you anywhere; apologizing sometimes does. And if someone does give in to your request, you can't thank him enough.

If you're invited to a Japanese home, you should know that it's both a rarity and an honor. Most Japanese consider their homes too small and humble for entertaining guests, which is why there are so many restaurants, coffee shops, and bars. If you're invited to a home, don't show up empty-handed. Bring a small gift such as candy, fruit, flowers, or perhaps a souvenir from your hometown. Alcohol is also appreciated. And if someone does extend you a favor, be sure to thank him again the next time you see him even if it's a year later.

Don't blow your nose in public if you can help it, and never at the dinner table. It's considered most disgusting. On the other hand, even though Japanese are very hygienic, they're not at all averse to spitting on the sidewalk. And, even more peculiar, the men urinate when and where they want, usually against a tree or a wall and most often after a night of carousing in the bars.

This being a man's society, men will walk in and out of doors and elevators before women, and in subways, they will sit down while women stand. Some Japanese men who have had contact with the

Western world (particularly hotel staff) will make a gallant show of allowing a Western woman to step out of the elevator first. For the sake of women living in Japan, thank them warmly.

Bowing The main form of greeting in Japan is the bow rather than the handshake. Although at first glance it may seem simple enough, the bow together with its implications is actually quite complicated. The depth of the bow and the number of seconds devoted to performing it, as well as the total number of bows, depend on who you are, to whom you're bowing, and how he's bowing back. In addition to bowing in greeting, Japanese also bow upon departing and to express gratitude. The proper form for a bow is to bend from the waist with a straight back and to keep your arms at your sides if you're a man or clasped in front of you if you're a woman, but if you're a foreigner, a simple nod of the head is enough. Knowing foreigners shake hands, a Japanese may extend his hand, although he probably won't be able to stop himself from giving a little bow as well. (I've even seen Japanese bow when talking on the telephone.) Although I've occasionally witnessed Japanese businessmen shaking hands among themselves, the practice is still quite rare. Kimono-clad hostesses of a high-end traditional Japanese inn will often kneel on *tatami* and bow to the ground as they send you off on your journey.

Visiting Card You're a nonentity in Japan if you don't have a visiting card, called a *meishi*. Everyone from housewives to bank presidents carries meishi to give out during introductions. If you're trying to conduct business in Japan, you'll be regarded suspiciously even as a phony if you don't have business cards. Meishi are very useful business tools for Japanese. Likewise, a meishi can be used as an introduction to a third party a Japanese may give you his meishi, scribble something on it, and tell you to present it to his cousin who owns a restaurant in Fukuoka. *Voilà* the cousin will treat you like a royal guest.

As a tourist, you don't have to have business cards, but it certainly doesn't hurt, and Japanese people will be greatly impressed by your preparedness. The card should have your address and occupation on it; you might even consider having your meishi made in Japan, with *katakana* (Japanese syllabic script) written on the reverse side.

Needless to say, there's a proper way to present a meishi. Turn it so that the other person can read it (that is, upside-down to you) and present it with both hands and a slight bow. If you are of equal status, you exchange meishi simultaneously; otherwise, the lower person on the totem pole presents the meishi first and delivers it underneath the card being received, to show deference. Afterward, don't simply put the meishi away. Rather, it's customary for both of you to study the meishi for a moment and, if possible, to comment on it (such as, "You're from Kyoto? My brother lived in Kyoto!" or "Sony! What a famous company!"). If you're at a business meeting, you should place the card in front of you on the table.

Shoes Nothing is so distasteful to Japanese as the soles of shoes. Therefore, you should take off your shoes before entering a home, a Japanese-style inn, a temple, and even some museums and restaurants. Usually, there will be plastic slippers at the entryway for you to slip on, but whenever you encounter *tatami,* you should take off even these slippers only bare feet or socks are allowed to tread upon tatami.

Restrooms present another set of slippers. If you're in a home or a Japanese inn, you'll notice another pair of slippers again plastic or rubber sitting right inside the restroom door. Step out of the hallway plastic shoes and into the bathroom slippers, and wear these the entire time you're in the restroom. When you're finished, change back into the hallway slippers. If you forget this last changeover, you'll regret it nothing is as embarrassing as walking into a room wearing toilet slippers and not realizing what you've done until you see the mixed looks of horror and mirth on the faces of Japanese people.

Bathing On my very first trip to Japan, I was certain I would never enter a Japanese bath. I was under the misconception that men and women bathed together, and I couldn't imagine getting into a tub with a group of smiling and bowing Japanese men. I needn't have worried in almost all circumstances, bathing is gender segregated. There are some exceptions, primarily at outdoor hot-spring spas in the countryside, but the women who go to these are usually grandmothers who couldn't care less. Young Japanese women wouldn't dream of jumping into a tub with a group of male strangers.

Japanese baths are delightful I'm addicted to them. You'll find them at Japanese-style inns, at *onsen* (hot-spring spas), and at *sento* (neighborhood baths); not everyone has his or her own bath in Japan. Sometimes they're elaborate affairs with indoor and outdoor tubs, and sometimes they're nothing more than a tiny tub. Public baths have long been regarded as social centers for Japanese friends and co-workers will visit hot-spring resorts together; neighbors exchange gossip at the neighborhood bath. Sadly, neighborhood baths have been in great decline over the past decades, as more and more Japanese acquire private baths. Hot-spring spas, however, remain hugely popular.

In any case, whether large or small, the procedure at all Japanese baths is the same. After completely disrobing in the changing room and putting your clothes in either a locker or a basket, hold a washcloth (provided free or available for sale at the bathhouse) in front of you so that it covers your vital parts and walk into the bathing area. There you'll find plastic basins and stools (sometimes they're still made of wood), and faucets along the wall. Sit on the stool in front of a faucet and repeatedly fill your basin with water (or use the hand-held faucet if available), splashing water all over you. If there's no hot water from the faucet, it's acceptable to dip your basin into the hot bath, but your washcloth should never touch the tub water. Rinsing yourself thoroughly is not only proper onsen manners; it also acclimatizes your body to the bath's hot temperature so you don't suffer a heart attack. While some Japanese just throw a bit of water over themselves, others soap down completely and I mean completely and then rinse away all traces of soap before getting into the tub. At any rate, only when you feel squeaky-clean should you enter the tub.

As in a Jacuzzi, everyone uses the same bath water. For that reason, you should never wash yourself in the tub, never put your washcloth into the bath (place it on your head or lay it beside the bath), and never pull the plug when you're done. After you bathe is when you scrub your body and wash your hair. I have never seen a group of people wash themselves so thoroughly as the Japanese, from their ears to their toes. All sento provide shampoo and body soap, along with interesting products provided free by companies hoping to rope in new customers, but in small public baths you might have to provide your own.

Your first attempt at a Japanese bath may be painful simply too scalding for comfort. It helps if you ease in gently and then sit perfectly still. You'll notice all tension and muscle stiffness ebbing away, a decidedly relaxing way to end the day. The Japanese are so fond of baths that many take them nightly, especially in winter when a hot bath keeps them toasty warm for hours. At an onsen, where hot-spring waters are considered curative, Japanese will bathe both at night and again in the morning, often making several trips between the faucet and the tubs and being careful not to rinse off the curative waters when they're done. With time, you'll probably become addicted, too. *Note:* Because tattoos in Japan have long been associated with *yakuza* (Japanese mafia), many public baths do not admit people with tattoos. However, if your tattoo is discreet and you're at, say, a small Japanese inn, you probably won't have any problems.

Cultural Briefing

Traditional Theatre

Kabuki Probably Japan's best-known traditional theater art, *kabuki* is also one of the country's most popular forms of entertainment. Visit a performance and it's easy to see why kabuki is fun! The plays are dramatic, the costumes are gorgeous, the stage settings are often fantastic, and the themes are universal love, revenge, and the conflict between duty and personal feelings. Probably one of the reasons kabuki is so popular even today is that it developed centuries ago as a form of entertainment for the common people in feudal Japan, particularly the merchants. And one of kabuki's interesting aspects is that all roles even those depicting women are portrayed by men.

Kabuki has changed little in the past 100-some years. Altogether there are more than 300 kabuki plays, all written before the 20th century. Kabuki stages almost always revolve and have an aisle that extends from the stage to the back of the spectator theater. For a Westerner, one of the more arresting things about a kabuki performance is the audience itself. Because this has always been entertainment for the masses, the audience can get quite lively with yells, guffaws, shouts of approval, and laughter. In fact, old woodcuts of cross-eyed men apparently stemmed from kabuki when things got a little too rowdy, actors would stamp their feet and strike a cross-eyed pose in an attempt to gain the audience's attention.

Of course, you won't be able to understand what's being said. Indeed, because much of kabuki drama dates from the 18th century, even Japanese sometimes have difficulty understanding the language. But it doesn't matter, though some theaters have English-language programs and earphones that describe the plots in minute detail. The best place to enjoy kabuki is Tokyo, where performances are held throughout much of the year.

Noh Whereas *kabuki* developed as a form of entertainment for the masses, Noh was a much more traditional and aristocratic form of theater. Most of Japan's shogun were patrons of Noh; during the Edo Period, it became the exclusive entertainment of the samurai class. In contrast to kabuki's extroverted liveliness, Noh is very calculated, slow, and restrained. The oldest form of theater in Japan, it has changed very little in the past 600 years, making it the oldest theater art in the world. The language is so archaic that Japanese cannot understand it at all, which explains in part why Noh does not have the popularity that kabuki does.

As in kabuki, all Noh performers are men, with the principal characters consisting mostly of ghosts or spirits, who illuminate foibles of human nature or tragic-heroic events. Performers often wear masks. Spoken parts are chanted by a chorus of about eight; music is provided by a Noh orchestra that consists of several drums and a flute.

Because the action is slow, watching an entire evening can be quite tedious unless you are particularly interested in Noh dance and music. In addition, most Noh plays do not have English translations. You may want to drop in for just a short while. In between Noh plays, short comic reliefs, called *kyogen,* usually make fun of life in the 1600s, depicting the lives of lazy husbands, conniving servants, and other characters with universal appeal.

Bunraku *Bunraku* is traditional Japanese puppet theater. But contrary to what you might expect, bunraku is for adults, and themes center on love and revenge, sacrifice and suicide. Many dramas now adapted for *kabuki* were first written for the bunraku stage.

Popular in Japan since the 17th century at times even more popular than kabuki bunraku is fascinating to watch because the puppeteers are right onstage with their puppets. Dressed in black, they're wonderfully skilled in making the puppets seem like living beings. Usually, there are three puppeteers for each puppet, which is about three-fourths human size: One puppeteer is responsible for movement of the puppet's head, as well as for the expression on its face, and for the movement of the right arm and hand; another puppeteer operates the puppet's left arm and hand; while the third moves the legs. Although at first the puppeteers are somewhat distracting, after a while you forget they're there as the puppets assume personalities of their own. The narrator, who tells the story and speaks the various parts, is an important figure in the drama. The narrator is accompanied by a traditional three-stringed Japanese instrument called a *shamisen*. By all means, try to see bunraku. The most famous presentations are at the Osaka Bunraku Theater, but there are performances in Tokyo and other major cities as well.

Sumo

The Japanese form of wrestling known as *sumo* began perhaps as long as 1,500 years ago and was immensely popular by the 6th century. Today it's still popular, with the best wrestlers revered as national heroes, much as baseball or basketball players are in the United States. Often taller than 1.8m (6 ft.) and weighing well over 136 kilograms (300 lb.), sumo wrestlers follow a rigorous training period, which usually begins when they're in their teens and includes eating special foods to gain weight. Unmarried wrestlers even live together at their training schools, called sumo stables.

A sumo match takes place on a sandy-floored ring less than 4.5m (15 ft.) in diameter. Wrestlers dress much as they did during the Edo

Period their hair in a samurai-style topknot, an ornamental belt/loincloth around their huge girths. Before each bout, the two contestants scatter salt in the ring to purify it from the last bout's loss; they also squat and then raise each leg, stamping it into the ground to crush, symbolically, any evil spirits. They then squat down and face each other, glaring to psych each other out. Once they rush each other, each wrestler's object is to either eject his opponent from the ring or cause him to touch the ground with any part of his body other than his feet. This is accomplished by shoving, slapping, tripping, throwing, and even carrying the opponent, but punching with a closed fist and kicking are not allowed. Altogether, there are 48 holds and throws, and sumo fans know all of them.

Most bouts are very short, lasting only 30 seconds or so. The highest-ranking players are called *yokozuna*, or grand champions; in 1993, a Hawaiian named Akebono was promoted to the highest rank, the first non-Japanese ever to be so honored. Nowadays foreign-born sumo wrestlers are common, though their numbers are restricted by the Japan Sumo Association.

There are six 15-day sumo tournaments in Japan every year: Three are held in Tokyo (Jan, May, and Sept); the others are held in Osaka (Mar), Nagoya (July), and Fukuoka (Nov). Each wrestler in the tournament faces a new opponent every day; the winner of the tournament is the wrestler who maintains the best overall record.

Tournament matches are also widely covered on television.

Tea Ceremony

Tea was brought to Japan from China more than 1,000 years ago. It first became popular among Buddhist priests as a means of staying awake during long hours of meditation; gradually, its use filtered down among the upper classes, and in the 16th century, the tea ceremony was perfected by a merchant named Sen-no-Rikyu. Using the principles of Zen and the spiritual discipline of the samurai, the tea ceremony became a highly stylized ritual, with detailed rules on how tea should be prepared, served, and drunk. The simplicity of movement and tranquillity of setting are meant to free the mind from the banality of everyday life and to allow the spirit to enjoy peace. In a way, it is a form of spiritual therapy.

The tea ceremony, *cha-no-yu,* is still practiced in Japan today and is regarded as a form of disciplinary training for mental composure and for etiquette and manners. In Kyoto, I once met a fellow guest in an inexpensive Japanese inn who asked whether she could serve me Japanese tea and a sweet after breakfast. She apologized for her ineptitude, saying she was only a mere apprentice of tea. When I asked how long she'd been studying cha-no-yu, she replied 7 years. That may seem like a long time, but the study of the tea ceremony includes related subjects, including the craftsmanship of tea vessels and implements, the design and construction of the teahouse, the landscaping of gardens, and literature related to the tea ceremony.

Several of Japan's more famous landscape gardens have teahouses on their grounds where you can sit on *tatami,* drink the frothy green tea (called *maccha*), eat sweets (meant to counteract the bitter taste of the tea), and contemplate the view. Traditionally, teahouses are quite small, with space for five or fewer people, and with two entrances: one for the host and the other for guests, so small that they must crawl through it to enter. In the center of the room is a small brazier for the teapot along with utensils needed for the making of tea tea bowl, tea caddy, bamboo whisk, and bamboo spoon. Tea etiquette requires that guests compliment the host on the excellent flavor of the tea and on the beauty of the tea implements, which of course change with the seasons and are often valuable art objects.

Although several first-class hotels in Tokyo hold tea ceremonies in special tea-ceremony rooms, nothing beats the atmosphere of a landscaped Japanese garden, many of which serve tea.

Floral & Landscape Arts

Ikebana Whereas a Westerner is likely to put a bunch of flowers into a vase and be done with it, Japanese consider the arrangement of flowers an art in itself. Most young girls have at least some training in flower arranging, known as *ikebana*. First popularized among aristocrats during the Heian Period (A.D. 794-1192) and spreading to the common people in the 14th to 16th centuries, traditional ikebana, in its simplest form, is supposed to represent heaven, man, and earth; it's considered a truly Japanese art without outside influences. As important as the arrangement itself is the vase chosen to display it. Department store galleries sometimes have ikebana exhibitions, as do shrines; otherwise, check with the local tourist office.

Gardens Nothing is left to chance in a Japanese landscape garden: The shapes of hills and trees, the placement of rocks and waterfalls everything is skillfully arranged in a faithful reproduction of nature. To Westerners, it may seem a bit strange to arrange nature to look like nature; but to Japanese, even nature can be improved upon to make it more pleasing through the best possible use of limited space. Japanese are masters at this, as a visit to any of their famous gardens will testify.

In fact, Japanese have been sculpting gardens for more than 1,000 years. At first, gardens were designed for walking and boating, with ponds, artificial islands, and pavilions. As with almost everything else in Japanese life, however, Zen Buddhism exerted an influence, making gardens simpler and attempting to create the illusion of boundless space within a small area. To the Buddhist, a garden was not for merriment but for contemplation an uncluttered and simple landscape on which to rest the eyes. Japanese gardens often use the principle of "borrowed landscape" that is, the incorporation of surrounding mountains and landscape into the overall design and impact of the garden.

Basically, there are three styles of Japanese gardens. One style, called tsukiyama, uses ponds, hills, and streams to depict nature in miniature. Another style, known as the karesansui, uses stones and raked sand in place of water and is often seen at Zen Buddhist temples; it was developed during the Muromachi Period as a representation of Zen spiritualism. The third style, called chaniwa, emerged with the tea ceremony; built around a teahouse with an eye toward simplicity and tranquillity, such a garden will often feature stone lanterns, a stone basin filled with water, or water flowing through a bamboo pipe.

Famous gardens in Japan include Kenrokuen Park in Kanazawa, Korakuen Park in Okayama, Ritsurin Park in Takamatsu, and the grounds of the Adachi Museum. Kyoto alone has about 50 gardens, including the famous Zen rock gardens at Daitokuji and Ryoanji temples, the gardens at both the Golden and Silver pavilions, and those at Heian Shrine, Nijo Castle, and the Katsura Imperial Villa.

Food & Drink

Whenever I leave Japan, it's the food I miss the most. Sure, there are sushi bars and other Japanese specialty restaurants in many major cities around the world, but they don't offer nearly the variety available in Japan (and often they aren't nearly as good). For just as America has more to offer than hamburgers and steaks and England more than fish and chips, Japan has more than just sushi and *teppanyaki.* For both the gourmet and the uninitiated, Japan is a treasure-trove of culinary surprises and a foodie's delight.

Japanese Cuisine

Altogether, there are more than a dozen different and distinct types of Japanese cuisine, plus countless regional specialties. A good deal of what you eat may be completely new to you as well as completely unidentifiable. Sometimes Japanese themselves don't even know what they're eating, so varied and so wide is the range of available edibles. The rule is simply to enjoy, and enjoyment begins even before you raise your chopsticks to your mouth.

To the Japanese, presentation of food is as important as the food itself, and dishes are designed to appeal not only to the palate but to the eye. In contrast to the American way of piling as much food as possible onto a single plate, Japanese use lots of small plates, each arranged artfully with bite-size morsels of food. After you've seen what can be done with maple leaves, flowers, bits of bamboo, and even pebbles to enhance the appearance of food, your relationship with what you eat may change forever. If there's such a thing as designer cuisine, Japan is its home.

Below are explanations of some of the most common types of Japanese cuisine. Generally, only one type of cuisine is served in a given restaurant for example, only raw seafood is served in a sushi bar, whereas tempura is featured at a tempura counter. There are exceptions to this, especially in regards to raw fish, which is served as an appetizer in many restaurants, and set meals, which contain a variety of dishes. In addition, Japanese restaurants in hotels may offer a great variety, and some Japanese drinking establishments (called *izakaya* or *nomiya*) offer a wide range of foods from soups to sushi to skewered pieces of chicken known as *yakitori*.

Fugu Known as blowfish, puffer fish, or globefish in English, *fugu* is one of the most exotic and adventurous foods in Japan: If it's not prepared properly, it means almost certain death for the consumer. Every year a few dozen people are hospitalized from fugu poisoning and a handful die, usually fishermen who tried preparing it at home. The fugu's ovaries and intestines are deadly and must be entirely removed without puncturing them. So why eat fugu if it can kill you? Well, for one thing, it's delicious; for another, fugu chefs are strictly licensed by the government and are greatly skilled in preparing fugu dishes. Ways to order it include *fugu-sashi* (raw), when it's sliced paper thin and dipped into soy sauce with bitter orange and chives; in *fugu-chiri* (stew) cooked with vegetables at your table; and as *fugu-zosui* (rice porridge). The season for fresh fugu is October or November through March, but some restaurants serve it throughout the year.

Kaiseki The king of Japanese cuisine, *kaiseki* is the epitome of delicately and exquisitely arranged food, the ultimate in Japanese aesthetic appeal. It's also among the most expensive meals you can eat and can cost ¥25,000 or more per person; some restaurants, however, do offer more affordable mini-kaiseki courses. In addition, the better Japanese inns serve kaiseki, a reason for their high cost. Kaiseki, which is not a specific dish but rather a complete meal, is expensive because much time and skill are involved in preparing each of the many dishes, with the ingredients cooked to preserve natural flavors. Even the plates are chosen with great care to enhance the color, texture, and shape of each piece of food.

Kaiseki cuisine is based on the four seasons, with the selection of ingredients and their presentation dependent on the time of the year. In fact, so strongly does a kaiseki preparation convey the mood of a particular season, the kaiseki gourmet could tell what season it is just by looking at a meal.

A kaiseki meal is usually a lengthy affair with various dishes appearing in set order. First come the appetizer, clear broth, and one uncooked dish. These are followed by boiled, broiled, fried, steamed, heated, and vinegary dishes and finally by another soup, rice, pickled vegetables, and fruit. Although meals vary greatly depending upon the region and what's fresh, common dishes include some type of sashimi, tempura, cooked seasonal fish, and bite-size pieces of various vegetables. Because kaiseki is always a set meal, there's no problem in ordering. Let your budget be your guide.

Kushiage Kushiage foods are breaded and deep-fried on skewers and include chicken, beef, seafood, and lots of seasonal vegetables (snow peas, green pepper, gingko nuts, lotus root, and the like). They're served with a slice of lemon and usually a specialty sauce. The result is delicious, and I highly recommend trying it. You'll find it at shops called *kushiage-ya* (*ya* means "shop"), which are often open only at night. Ordering the set meal is easiest, and what you get is often determined by both the chef and the season.

Okonomiyaki *Okonomiyaki,* which originated in Osaka after World War II and literally means "as you like it," is often referred to as Japanese pizza. To me, it's more like a pancake to which meat or fish, shredded cabbage, and vegetables are added, topped with Worcestershire sauce. Because it's a popular offering of street vendors, restaurants specializing in this type of cuisine are very reasonably priced. At some places the cook makes it for you, but at other places it's do-it-yourself, which can be quite fun if you're with a group. *Yakisoba* (fried Chinese noodles with cabbage) is also usually offered at okonomiyaki restaurants.

Rice As in other Asian countries, rice has been a Japanese staple for about 2,000 years. In fact, rice is so important to the Japanese diet that *gohan* means both "rice" and "meal." There are no problems here everyone is familiar with rice. The difference, however, is that in Japan it's quite sticky, making it easier to pick up with chopsticks. It's also just plain white rice no salt, no butter, no soy sauce (it's thought to be rather uncouth to dump a lot of sauces in your rice) though trendy restaurants may sprinkle rice bowls with black sesame seeds, plum powder, or other seasoning. In the old days, not everyone could afford the expensive white kind, which was grown primarily to pay taxes or rent to the feudal lord; peasants had to be satisfied with a mixture of brown rice, millet, and greens. Today, some Japanese still eat rice three times a day, although they're now just as apt to have bread and coffee for breakfast. Restaurants specializing in organic foods often offer *genmai* (unpolished brown rice).

Robatayaki *Robatayaki* refers to restaurants in which seafood and vegetables are cooked over an open charcoal grill. In the olden days, an *robata* (open fireplace) in the middle of an old Japanese house was the center of activity for cooking, eating, socializing, and simply keeping warm. Therefore, today's robatayaki restaurants are like nostalgia trips back into Japan's past and are often decorated in rustic farmhouse style with the staff dressed in traditional clothing. Robatayaki restaurants mostly open only in the evening are popular among office workers for both eating and drinking.

There's no special menu in a robatayaki restaurant rather, it includes just about everything eaten in Japan. The difference is that most of the food will be grilled. Favorites of mine include *ginnan* (gingko nuts), asparagus wrapped in bacon, *piman* (a type of green pepper), mushrooms (various kinds), *jagabataa* (potatoes), and just about any kind of fish. You can usually get skewers of beef or chicken as well as *nikujaga* (a stew of meat and potatoes) delicious during cold winter months. Because ordering is often a la carte, you'll just have to look and point.

Sashimi & Sushi It's estimated that the average Japanese eats 38 kilograms (84 lb.) of seafood a year that's six times the average American consumption. Although this seafood may be served in any number of ways from grilled to boiled, a great deal of it is eaten raw.

Sashimi is simply raw seafood, usually served as an appetizer and eaten alone (that is, without rice). If you've never eaten it, a good choice to start out with is *maguro,* or lean tuna, which doesn't taste fishy at all and is so delicate in texture that it almost melts in your mouth. The way to eat sashimi is to first put *wasabi* (pungent green horseradish) into a small dish of soy sauce and then dip the raw fish in the sauce using your chopsticks (some purists maintain that wasabi and soy sauce shouldn't be mixed, but that's what my Japanese friends do).

Sushi, which is raw fish with vinegared rice, comes in many varieties. The best known is *nigiri-zushi:* raw fish, seafood, or vegetables placed on top of vinegared rice with just a touch of wasabi. It's also dipped in soy sauce. Use chopsticks or your fingers to eat sushi; remember you're supposed to eat each piece in one bite quite a mouthful, but about the only way to keep it from falling apart. Another trick is to turn it upside down when you dip it in the sauce, to keep the rice from crumbling.

Also popular is *maki-zushi,* which consists of seafood, vegetables, or pickles rolled with rice inside a sheet of *nori* seaweed. *Inari-zushi* is vinegared rice and chopped vegetables inside a pouch of fried tofu bean curd.

Typical sushi includes *maguro* (tuna), *hirame* (flounder), *tai* (sea bream), *ika* (squid), *tako* (octopus), *ebi* (shrimp), *anago* (sea eel), and *tamago* (omelet). Ordering is easy because you usually sit at a counter where you can see all the food in a refrigerated glass case in front of you. You also get to see the sushi chefs at work. The typical meal begins with sashimi and is followed by sushi, but if you don't want to order separately, there are always various *seto* (set meals or courses). Pickled ginger is part of any sushi meal.

By the way, the least expensive sushi is *chirashi,* which is a selection of fish, seafood, and usually tamago on a large shallow bowl of rice. Because you get more rice, those of you with bigger appetites may want to order chirashi. Another way to enjoy sushi without spending a fortune is at a *kaiten* sushi shop, in which plates of sushi circulate on a conveyor belt on the counter customers reach for the dishes they want and pay for the number of dishes they take.

Shabu-Shabu & Sukiyaki Until the Meji Restoration beginning in 1868, which brought foreigners to Japan, Japanese could think of nothing as disgusting as eating the flesh of animals (fish was okay). Meat was considered unclean by Buddhists, and consuming it was banned by the emperor way back in the 7th century. Imagine the horror of Japanese when they discovered that Western "barbarians" ate bloody meat! It wasn't until Emperor Meiji himself announced his intention to eat meat that Japanese accepted the idea. Today, Japanese have become skilled in preparing a number of beef dishes.

Sukiyaki is among Japan's best-known beef dishes and is one many Westerners seem to prefer. Whenever I'm invited to a Japanese home, this is the meal most often served. Like fondue, it's cooked at the table.

Sukiyaki is thinly sliced beef cooked in a broth of soy sauce, stock, and sake along with scallions, spinach, mushrooms, tofu, bamboo shoots, and other vegetables. All diners serve themselves from the simmering pot and then dip their morsels into their own bowl of raw egg. You can skip the raw egg if you want (most Westerners do), but it adds to the taste and also cools the food down enough so that it doesn't burn.

Shabu-shabu is also prepared at your table and consists of thinly sliced beef cooked in a broth with vegetables in a kind of Japanese fondue. (It's named for the swishing sound the beef supposedly makes when cooking.) The main difference between the two dishes is the broth: Whereas in sukiyaki it consists of stock flavored with soy sauce and sake and is slightly sweet, in shabu-shabu it's relatively clear and has little taste of its own. The pots used are also different.

Using their chopsticks, *shabu* diners submerge pieces of meat in the watery broth until they're cooked. This usually takes only a few seconds. Vegetables are left in longer to swim around until fished out. For dipping, there's either sesame sauce with diced green onions or a more bitter fish stock sauce. Restaurants serving sukiyaki usually serve shabu-shabu as well, and they're usually happy to show you the right way to prepare and eat it.

Shojin Ryori Shojin Ryori is the ultimate vegetarian meal, created centuries ago to serve the needs of Zen Buddhist priests and pilgrims. Dishes may include *yudofu*(simmered tofu) and an array of local vegetables. Kyoto is the best place to experience this type of cuisine.

Soba & Udon Noodles Japanese love eating noodles, but I suspect at least part of the fascination stems from the way they eat them they slurp, sucking in the noodles with gravity-defying speed. What's more, slurping noodles is considered proper etiquette. Fearing it would stick with me forever, however, slurping is a technique I've never quite mastered.

There are many different kinds of noodles, and it seems like almost every region of Japan has its own special style or kind some are eaten plain, some in combination with other foods such as shrimp tempura, some served hot, some served cold. *Soba,*made from unbleached buckwheat flour and enjoyed for its nutty flavor and high nutritional value, is eaten hot *(kake-soba)* or cold *(zaru-soba). Udon* is a thick white wheat noodle originally from Osaka; it's usually served hot. *Somen* is a fine white noodle eaten cold in the summer and dunked in a cold sauce. Establishments serving noodles range from stand-up eateries to more refined noodle restaurants with *tatami*seating. Regardless of where you eat them, noodles are among the least expensive dishes in Japan.

Tempura Today a well-known Japanese food, tempura was actually introduced by the Portuguese in the 16th century. Tempura is fish and vegetables coated in a batter of egg, water, and wheat flour and then deep-fried; it's served piping hot. To eat it, dip it in a sauce of soy, fish stock, *daikon* (radish), and grated ginger; in some restaurants, only some salt, powdered green tea, or a lemon wedge is provided as an accompaniment. Various tempura specialties may include *nasu* (eggplant), *shiitake* (mushroom), *satsumaimo* (sweet potato), *shishito* (small green pepper), *renkon* (sliced lotus root), *ebi* (shrimp), *ika* (squid), *shisho* (lemon-mint leaf), and many kinds of fish. Again, the easiest thing to do is to order the *teishoku* (set meal).

Teppanyaki A *teppanyaki* restaurant is a Japanese steakhouse. As in the famous Benihana restaurants in many U.S. cities, the chef slices, dices, and cooks your meal of tenderloin or sirloin steak and vegetables on a smooth, hot grill right in front of you though with much less fanfare than his U.S. counterpart. Because beef is relatively new in Japanese cooking, some people categorize teppanyaki restaurants as "Western." However, I consider this style of cooking and presentation special enough to be referred to as Japanese. Teppanyaki restaurants also tend to be expensive, simply because of the price of beef in Japan, with Kobe beef the most prized.

Tofu Originally from China, tofu, or bean curd, is made from soy milk. It has little flavor of its own and is served cold in summer and *yudofu* (boiled) in winter. A byproduct of tofu is *yuba,* thin sheets rich in protein.

Tonkatsu *Tonkatsu* is the Japanese word for "pork cutlet," made by dredging pork in wheat flour, moistening it with egg and water, dipping it in bread crumbs, and deep-frying it in vegetable oil. Because tonkatsu restaurants are generally inexpensive, they're popular with office workers and families. It's easiest to order the *teishoku,* which usually features either the *hirekatsu* (pork filet) or the *rosukatsu* (pork loin). In any case, tonkatsu is served on a bed of shredded cabbage, and one or two different sauces will be at your table, a Worcestershire sauce and perhaps a specialty sauce. If you order the teishoku, it will come with rice, miso soup, and pickled vegetables. Pork cutlet served on a bowl of rice is *katsudon.*

Unagi I'll bet that if you eat *unagi* without knowing what it is, you'll find it very tasty and you'll probably be very surprised to find out you've just eaten eel. Popular as a health food because of its rich protein and high vitamin A content, eel is supposed to help you fight fatigue during hot summer months but is eaten year-round. *Kabayaki*(broiled eel) is prepared by grilling filet strips over a charcoal fire; the eel is repeatedly dipped in a sweetened barbecue soy sauce while cooking. A favorite way to eat broiled eel is on top of rice, in which case it's called *unaju* or *unagi donburi*. Do yourself a favor and try it.

Yakitori *Yakitori* is chunks of chicken or chicken parts basted in a sweet soy sauce and grilled over a charcoal fire on thin skewers. Places that specialize in yakitori (*yakitori-ya,* often identifiable by a red paper lantern outside the front door) are technically not restaurants but drinking establishments; they usually don't open until 5 or 6pm. Most yakitori-ya are popular with workers as inexpensive places to drink, eat, and be merry.

The cheapest way to dine on yakitori is to order a set course, which will often include various parts of the chicken including the skin, heart, and liver. If this isn't entirely to your taste, you may wish to order a la carte, which is more expensive but gets you exactly what you want. In addition to chicken, other skewered, charcoaled delicacies are usually offered (called *kushi-yaki*). If you're ordering by the stick, you might want to try *sasami* (chicken breast), *tsukune* (chicken meatballs), *piman* (green peppers), *negima* (chicken and leeks), *shiitake* (mushrooms), or *ginnan* (gingko nuts).

Other Cuisines During your travels you might also run into these types of Japanese cuisine: *Kamameshi* is a rice casserole served in individual-size cast-iron pots with different toppings that might include seafood, meat, or vegetables. *Donburi* is also a rice dish, topped with tempura, eggs, and meat such as chicken or pork. *Nabe,* a stew cooked in an earthenware pot at your table, consists of chicken, sliced beef, pork, or seafood; noodles; and vegetables. *Oden* is a broth with fish cakes, tofu, eggs, and vegetables, served with hot mustard. If a restaurant advertises that it specializes in *Kyodo-Ryori,* it serves local specialties for which the region is famous and is often very rustic in decor. A more recent trend is crossover fusion cuisine creative dishes inspired by ingredients from both sides of the Pacific. Upmarket *izakaya* may also serve nouvelle dishes.

Although technically considered Chinese fast-food restaurants, ramen shops are a big part of dining in Japan. Serving what I consider to be generic Chinese noodles, soups, and other dishes, ramen shops can be found everywhere; they're easily recognizable by red signs and often pictures of various dishes displayed right by the front door. Many are stand-up affairs just a high counter to rest your bowl on. In addition to *ramen* (noodle and vegetable soup), you can also get such things as *yakisoba* (fried noodles) or my favorite *gyoza* (fried pork dumplings). What these places lack in atmosphere is made up for in price: Dishes average less than ¥700, making them some of the cheapest places in Japan for a meal.

Drinks

All Japanese restaurants serve complimentary green tea with meals. If that's too weak, you might want to try sake (also known as *nihonshu*), an alcoholic beverage made from rice and served either hot or cold. It goes well with most forms of Japanese cuisine. Produced since about the 3rd century, sake varies by region, production method, alcoholic content, color, aroma, and taste. There are more than 1,800 sake brewers in Japan producing about 10,000 varieties. Miyabi is a prized classic sake; other brands are Gekkeikan, Koshinokanbai, Hakutsuru (meaning White Crane), and Ozeki. A good place to try a good variety of sake is at a Japanese-style pub, an *izakaya*.

Japanese beer is also very popular. The biggest sellers are Kirin, Sapporo, Asahi, and Suntory, with each brand offering a bewildering variety of brews. They enjoyed exclusive brewing rights until deregulation in the 1990s opened the gates to competition; now microbreweries are found everywhere in Japan. Businessmen are fond of whiskey, which they usually drink with ice and water. Popular in recent years is *shochu,* a clear, distilled spirit usually made from rice but sometimes from wheat, sweet potatoes, barley, or sugar cane. It used to be considered a drink of the lower classes, but sales have increased so much that it's threatening the sake and whiskey businesses. A clear liquid comparable, perhaps, to vodka, it can be consumed straight but is often combined with soda water in a drink called *chuhai.* My personal favorite is *ume-shu,* a plum-flavored shochu. But watch out the stuff can be deadly. Wine, usually available only at restaurants serving Western food, has gained in popularity in recent years, with both domestic and imported brands available. Although cocktailsare available in dance clubs, hotel lounges, and fancier bars at rather inflated prices, most Japanese stick with beer, wine, sake, shochu, or whiskey.

History
Ancient History (ca. 30,000 B.C.-A.D. 710)
According to mythology, Japan's history began when the sun goddess, Amaterasu, sent one of her descendants down to the island of Kyushu to unify the people of Japan. Unification, however, was not realized until a few generations later when Jimmu, the great-grandson of the goddess's emissary, succeeded in bringing all of the country under his

rule. Because of his divine descent, Jimmu became emperor in 660 B.C. (the date is mythical), thus establishing the line from which all of Japan's emperors are said to derive. However mysterious the origin of this imperial dynasty, it is acknowledged as the longest reigning such family in the world.

Legend begins to give way to fact only in the 4th century A.D., when a family by the name of Yamato succeeded in expanding its kingdom throughout much of the country. At the core of the unification achieved by the Yamato family was the Shinto religion. Indigenous to Japan, Shintoism is marked by the worship of natural things mountains, trees, stars, rivers, seas, fire, animals, even vegetables as the embodiment of *kami* (gods) and of the spirits of ancestors. It is also marked by belief in the emperor's divinity. Along with Buddhism, Shintoism is still a driving belief in Japanese life.

Although the exact origin of Japanese people is unknown, we know Japan was once connected to the Asian mainland by a land bridge, and the territory of Japan was occupied as early as 30,000 B.C. From about 10,000 B.C. to 400 B.C., hunter-gatherers, called Jomon, thrived in small communities primarily in central Honshu; they're best known for their hand-formed pottery decorated with cord patterns. The Jomon Period was followed by the Yayoi Period, which was marked by metalworking, the pottery wheel, and the mastering of irrigated rice cultivation. The Yayoi Period lasted until about A.D. 300, after which the Yamato family unified the state for the first time and set up their court in what is now Nara Prefecture. Yamato (present-day Japan) began turning cultural feelers toward its great neighbor to the west, China.

In the 6th century, Buddhism, which originated in India, was brought to Japan via China and Korea, followed by the importation of Chinese cultural and scholarly knowledge including art, architecture, and the use of Chinese written characters. In 604, the prince regent Shotoku, greatly influenced by the teachings of Buddhism and Confucianism and still a beloved figure today, drafted a document calling for political reforms and a constitutional government. By 607, he was sending Japanese scholars to China to study Buddhism, and he started building Buddhist temples. The most famous is Horyuji Temple near Nara, said to be the oldest existing wooden structure in the world. He also built Shitennoji Temple in what is now Osaka.

The Nara Period (710-84)

Before the 700s, the site of Japan's capital changed every time a new emperor came to the throne. In 710, however, a permanent capital was established at Nara. Although it remained the capital for only 74 years, seven successive emperors ruled from Nara. The period was graced with the expansion of Buddhism and flourishing temple construction throughout the country. Buddhism also inspired the arts, including Buddhist sculpture, metal casting, painting, and lacquerware. It was during this time that Emperor Shomu, the most devout Buddhist among the Nara emperors, ordered the casting of a huge bronze statue of Buddha to be erected in Nara. Known as the Daibutsu, it remains Nara's biggest attraction.

The Heian Period (794-1192)

In 794, the capital was moved to Heiankyo (present-day Kyoto), and following the example of cities in China, Kyoto was laid out in a grid pattern with broad roads and canals. Heiankyo means "capital of peace and tranquillity," and the Heian Period was a glorious time for aristocratic families, a time of luxury and prosperity during which court life reached new artistic heights. Moon viewing became popular. Chinese characters were blended with a new Japanese writing system, allowing for the first time the flowering of Japanese literature and poetry. The life of the times was captured in the works of two women: Sei Shonagon, who wrote a collection of impressions of her life at court known as the *Pillow Book;* and Murasaki Shikibu, who wrote the world's first major novel, *The Tale of Genji.*

Because the nobles were completely engrossed in their luxurious lifestyles, however, they failed to notice the growth of military clans in the provinces. The two most powerful warrior clans were the Taira (also called Heike) and the Minamoto (also called Genji), whose fierce civil wars tore the nation apart until a young warrior, Minamoto Yoritomo, established supremacy. (In Japan, a person's family name here, Minamoto comes first, followed by the given name; I have followed this order throughout this book.)

The Kamakura Period (1192-1333)

Wishing to set up rule far away from Kyoto, Minamoto Yoritomo established his capital in a remote and easily defended fishing village called Kamakura, not far from today's Tokyo. In becoming the nation's first shogun, or military dictator, Minamoto Yoritomo laid the groundwork for 700 years of military governments in which the power of the country passed from the aristocratic court into the hands of the warrior class until the imperial court was restored in 1868.

The Kamakura Period is perhaps best known for the unrivaled ascendancy of the warrior caste, or samurai. Ruled by a rigid honor code, samurai were bound in loyalty to their feudal lord, and they became the only caste allowed to carry two swords. They were expected to give up their lives for their lord without hesitation, and if they failed in their duty, they could regain their honor only by committing ritualistic suicide, or *seppuku*. Spurning the soft life led by court nobles, samurai embraced a spartan lifestyle. When Zen Buddhism, with its tenets of mental and physical discipline, was introduced into Japan from China in the 1190s, it appealed greatly to the samurai. Weapons and armor achieved new heights in artistry, while *Bushido,* the way of the warrior, contributed to the spirit of national unity.

In 1274, Mongolian forces under Kublai Khan made an unsuccessful attempt to invade Japan. They returned in 1281 with a larger fleet, but a typhoon destroyed it. Regarding the cyclone as a gift from the gods, Japanese called it *kamikaze,* meaning "divine wind," which took on a different significance at the end of World War II when Japanese pilots flew suicide missions in an attempt to turn the tide of war.

The Muromachi & Azuchi-Momoyama Periods (1336-1603)

After the fall of the Kamakura shogunate, a new feudal government was set up at Muromachi in Kyoto. The next 200 years, however, were marred by bloody civil wars as *daimyo* (feudal lords) staked out their fiefdoms. Similar to the barons of Europe, the daimyo owned tracts of land, had complete rule over the people who lived on them, and had an army of retainers, the samurai, who fought his enemies. This period of civil wars is called Sengoku-Jidai, or Age of the Warring States.

Yet these centuries of strife also saw a blossoming of art and culture. Kyoto witnessed the construction of the extravagant Golden and Silver pavilions as well as the artistic arrangement of Ryoanji Temple's famous rock garden. Noh drama, the tea ceremony, flower arranging, and landscape gardening became the passions of the upper class. At the end of the 16th century, a number of castles were built on mountaintops to demonstrate the strength of the daimyo, guard their fiefdoms, and defend themselves against the firearms introduced by the Portuguese.

In the second half of the 16th century, a brilliant military strategist by the name of Oda Nobunaga almost succeeded in ending the civil wars. Upon Oda's assassination by one of his own retainers, one of his best generals, Toyotomi Hideyoshi, took up the campaign, built magnificent Osaka Castle, and crushed rebellion to unify Japan. Oda and Toyotomi's successive rules are known as the Azuchi-Momoyama Period, after the names of their castles.

The Edo Period (1603-1867)

Upon Toyotomi's death (1598), power was seized by Tokugawa Ieyasu, a statesman so shrewd and skillful in eliminating enemies that his heirs would continue to rule Japan for the next 250 years. After defeating his greatest rival in the famous battle of Sekigahara, Tokugawa set up a shogunate government in 1603 in Edo (present-day Tokyo), leaving the emperor intact but virtually powerless in Kyoto. In 1615, the Tokugawa government assured its supremacy by getting rid of Toyotomi's descendants in a fierce battle at Osaka Castle that destroyed the castle and annihilated the Toyotomi clan.

Meanwhile, European influence in Japan was spreading. The first contact with the Western world had occurred in 1543, when Portuguese merchants (with firearms) arrived, followed by Christian missionaries. St. Francis Xavier landed in Kyushu in 1549, remaining for 2 years and converting thousands of Japanese; by 1580, there were perhaps as many as 150,000 Japanese Christians. Although Japan's rulers at first welcomed foreigners and trade (three Kyushu daimyo even went so far as to send emissaries to Rome, where they were received by the pope), they gradually became alarmed by the Christian missionary influence. Hearing of the Catholic Church's power in Rome and fearing the expansionist policies of European nations, Toyotomi banned Christianity in the late 1500s. In 1597, 26 Japanese and European Christians were crucified in Nagasaki.

The Tokugawa shogunate intensified the campaign against Christians in 1639 when it closed all ports to foreign trade. Adopting a policy of total isolation, the shogunate forbade foreigners from landing in Japan and Japanese from leaving; even Japanese who had been living abroad in overseas trading posts were never allowed to return. The only exception was in Nagasaki, home to a colony of tightly controlled Chinese merchants and a handful of Dutch confined to a tiny island trading post.

Thus began an amazing 215-year period in Japanese history during which Japan was closed to the rest of the world. It was a time of political stability at the expense of personal freedom, as all aspects of life were strictly controlled by the Tokugawa government. Japanese society was divided into four distinct classes: samurai, farmers, craftspeople, and merchants. Class determined everything in daily life, from where a person could live to what he was allowed to wear or eat. Samurai led the most exalted social position, and it was probably during the Tokugawa Period that the samurai class reached the zenith of its glory.

At the bottom of the social ladder were the merchants, but as they prospered under the peaceful regime, new forms of entertainment arose to occupy their time. Kabuki drama and woodblock prints became the rage, while stoneware and porcelain, silk brocade for kimono, and lacquerware improved in quality. In fact, it was probably the shogunate's rigid policies that actually fostered the arts. Because anything new was considered dangerous and quickly suppressed, Japanese were forced to retreat inward, focusing their energies in the arts and perfecting handicrafts down to the minutest detail whether it was swords, kimono, or lacquered boxes. Only Japan's many festivals and pilgrimages to designated religious sites offered relief from harsh and restrictive social mores.

To ensure that no daimyo in the distant provinces would become too powerful and a threat to the shogun's power, the Tokugawa government ordered each daimyo to leave his family in Edo as permanent residents (effectively as hostages) and required the lord to spend a prescribed number of months in Edo every year or two. Inns and townships sprang up along Japan's major highways to accommodate the elaborate processions of palanquins, samurai, and footmen traveling back and forth between Edo and the provinces. In expending so much time and money traveling back and forth and maintaining elaborate residences both in the provinces and in Edo, the daimyo had no resources left with which to wage a rebellion.

Yet even though the Tokugawa government took such extreme measures to ensure its supremacy, by the mid-19th century it was clear that the feudal system was outdated and economic power had shifted into the hands of the merchants. Many samurai families were impoverished, and discontent with the shogunate became widespread.

In 1853, American Commodore Matthew C. Perry sailed to Japan, seeking to gain trading rights. He left unsuccessful, but returning a year later he forced the Shogun to sign an agreement despite the disapproval of the emperor, thus ending Japan's 2 centuries of isolation. In 1867, powerful families toppled the Tokugawa regime and restored the emperor as ruler, thus bringing the Feudal Era to a close.

Meiji Period Through World War II (1868-1945)

In 1868, Emperor Meiji moved his imperial government from Kyoto to Edo, renamed it Tokyo (Eastern Capital), and designated it the official national capital. During the next few decades, known as the Meiji Restoration, Japan rapidly progressed from a feudal agricultural society of samurai and peasants to an industrial nation.

The samurai were stripped of their power and no longer allowed to carry swords, thus ending a privileged way of life begun almost 700 years earlier in Kamakura. A prime minister and a cabinet were appointed, a constitution was drafted, and a parliament (called the Diet) was elected. With the enthusiastic support of Emperor Meiji, the latest in Western technological know-how was imported, including railway and postal systems, along with specialists and advisers: Between 1881 and 1898, about 10,000 Westerners were retained by the Japanese government to help modernize the country.

Meanwhile, Japan made incursions into neighboring lands. In 1894 to 1895, it fought and won a war against China; in 1904 to 1905, it attacked and defeated Russia; and in 1910, it annexed Korea. After militarists gained control of the government in the 1930s, these expansionist policies continued; Manchuria was annexed, and Japan went to war with China again in 1937. On the other side of the world, as World War II flared in Europe, Japan formed a military alliance (Axis) with Germany and Italy and attacked French Indochina.

After several years of tense diplomatic confrontations between Japan and America, Japanese extremists decided to attack Pearl Harbor in the hope that by striking first they could prevent U.S. mobilization. On December 7, 1941, Japan bombed Pearl Harbor, entering World War II against the United States. Although Japan went on to conquer Hong Kong, Singapore, Burma, Malaysia, the Philippines, the Dutch East

Indies, and Guam, the tide eventually turned, and American bombers reduced every major Japanese city to rubble with the exception of historic Kyoto.

On August 6, 1945, the United States dropped the world's first atomic bomb over Hiroshima, followed on August 9 by a second over Nagasaki. Japan submitted to unconditional surrender on August 14, with Emperor Hirohito's radio broadcast telling his people the time had come for "enduring the unendurable and suffering what is insufferable." American and other Allied occupation forces arrived and remained until 1952. For the first time in history, Japan had suffered defeat by a foreign power; the country had never before been invaded or occupied by a foreign nation.

Modern Japan (1946-Present)

The experience of World War II had a profound effect on the Japanese, yet they emerged from their defeat and began to rebuild. In 1946, under the guidance of the Allied military authority headed by U.S. Gen. Douglas MacArthur, they adopted a democratic constitution renouncing war and the use of force to settle international disputes and divesting the emperor of divinity. A parliamentary system of government was set up, and 1947 witnessed the first general elections for the National Diet, the government's legislative body. After its founding in 1955, the Liberal Democratic Party (LDP) remained the undisputed majority party for decades, giving Japan the political stability it needed to grow economically and compete in world markets.

To the younger generation, the occupation was less a painful burden to be suffered than an opportunity to remake their country, with American encouragement, into a modern, peace-loving, and democratic state. A relationship developed between Japanese and their American occupiers. In the early 1950s, as the Cold War between the United States and the Communist world erupted in hostilities in Korea, that relationship grew into a firm alliance, strengthened by a security treaty. In 1952, the occupation ended, and Japan joined the United Nations as an independent country.

Avoiding involvement in foreign conflicts as outlined by its constitution, Japanese concentrated on economic recovery. Through a series of policies favoring domestic industries and shielding Japan from foreign competition, they achieved rapid economic growth. In 1964, Tokyo hosted the Summer Olympic Games, showing the world that the nation had transformed itself into a formidable industrialized power. Incomes doubled during the 1960s, and a 1967 government study found that 90% of Japanese considered themselves middle class.

By the 1980s, Japan was by far the richest industrialized nation in Asia and the envy of its neighbors, who strove to emulate Japan's success. Sony was a household word around the globe; books flooded the international market touting the economic secrets of Japan, Inc. After all, Japan seemed to have it all: a good economy, political stability, safe streets, and great schools. As the yen soared, Japanese traveled abroad as never before, and Japanese companies gained international attention as they gobbled up real estate in foreign lands and purchased works of art at unheard-of prices.

Meanwhile, a snowballing trade surplus had created friction between Japan and the United States, its chief trading partner. In the 1980s, as Japanese auto sales in the United States soared and foreign sales in Japan continued to be restricted, disagreements between Tokyo and Washington heated up. In 1989, Emperor Hirohito died of cancer at age 87, bringing the 63-year Showa Era to an end and ushering in the Heisei Period under Akihito, the 125th emperor, who proclaimed the new "Era of Peace" (Heisei).

In the early 1990s, shadows of financial doubt began to spread over the Land of the Rising Sun, with alarming reports of bad bank loans, inflated stock prices, and overextended corporate investment abroad. In 1992, recession hit Japan, bursting the economic bubble and plunging the country into its worst recession since World War II. The Nikkei (the Japanese version of the American Dow) fell a gut-churning 63% from its 1989 peak, and, over the next decade, bankruptcies reached an all-time high and unemployment climbed to its highest level since World War II. Meanwhile, the Liberal Democratic Party, which had held power uninterruptedly for nearly 4 decades, suffered a huge loss of public confidence after its top officials were accused of participating in a series of political and financial scandals. But a revolving door of prime ministers (many of whom also became implicated in scandals) throughout the 1990s failed to revive the economy or alleviate voters' growing fears of financial doom.

Public confidence was further eroded in 1995, first by a major earthquake in Kobe that killed more than 6,000 people and proved that Japan's cities were not as safe as the government had maintained. Then an attack by an obscure religious sect that released the deadly nerve gas sarin on Tokyo's subway system during rush hour killed 12 people and sickened thousands. But the worst blow was in 2001, when a knife-wielding man fatally stabbed eight children in an elementary school in Osaka Prefecture. For many Japanese, it seemed that the very core of their society had begun to crumble.

In April 2001, after yet another prime minister resigned due to scandal, Koizumi Junichiro took the political helm. Although a member of the LPD, the long-haired, 59-year-old Koizumi, who enjoyed popularity usually reserved for rock stars, had long been considered something of a maverick, battling against the long-established power brokers of the LPD. Following the September 2001 terrorist attacks in the U.S., Koizumi quickly showed allegiance by pushing through an antiterrorism bill that allowed noncombat support in Afghanistan, followed by a pledge of foreign aid to American reconstruction efforts in Iraq.

Koizumi's greatest domestic achievements were policies that nudged Japan's slow climb out of recession, including those that cut the number of bad bank loans in half and laid groundwork for the privatization of Japan's post office, which does far more than sell stamps and deliver mail. Tokyo real estate prices, which had fallen as much as 70% from their 1991 peak, rose for the first time in 2004, spurring investors to return. By 2008, a slew of international luxury hotels had muscled their way into the Tokyo market, while new urban-renewal projects had reshaped the Tokyo skyline.

On the international front, Japan's most immediate worry continued to be its neighbor, North Korea, which lobbed its first missile over

Japan in 1998, declared in 2002 that it had never halted its nuclear-weapons program despite a 1994 nuclear accord, and in 2008 launched its first satellite rocket over Japan. In 2002, North Korea admitted that it had abducted 13 young Japanese in the '70s and '80s to teach its spies the Japanese language and customs. Five of the abductees were subsequently repatriated back to Japan; North Korea maintains the others died of natural causes.

In 1999, Japan, which did not have a legally recognized national flag nor an anthem, adopted a World War II hymn, *Kimigayo,* as its national anthem and declared the traditional Japanese sun flag, a red disk in a field of white, its official flag. But any overt displays of Japanese nationalism have always spurred criticism from Asian neighbors, who maintain that despite an official apology in 1995 for wartime aggression, Japan has never truly shown remorse for invading and occupying its neighbors. Prime ministers and other officials have repeatedly outraged fellow Asians with visits to Tokyo's Yasukuni Shrine, vilified by critics for honoring Japanese war dead, including those executed for wartime atrocities.

Relations became further strained in 2005, when Japan's Education Ministry approved revised history textbooks that glossed over Japan's war crimes, sparking outrage in China and South Korea that erupted into anti-Japanese street riots. In 2007, an international furor arose when Abe Shinzo, who had replaced Koizumi as prime minister, claimed that no evidence existed of women being forced to work in Asian brothels established by Japanese military during World War II. Abe, who at 52 was Japan's youngest postwar premier, lasted only a year; his two successors fared little better.

Although Japan, whose foremost trading partner had shifted from the United States to China, seemed to be on the economic mend by the mid-2000s, the 2008 global financial meltdown hijacked its recovery by causing a downward spiral in foreign trade as demand for Japanese cars, electronics, and other exports dropped dramatically around the world. Sony, Toyota, Panasonic, Sharp, and other major companies were forced to dramatically curtail production and close plants, causing thousands of workers to lose their jobs.

By mid-2009 the jobless rate was 5.7%, its highest postwar level. Many of the newly unemployed, forced from company-sponsored housing or unable to pay rent, joined the ranks of the homeless, estimated in 2009 at about 15,800. In 2010, grim news about two world-famous Japanese companies added to a growing sense of gloom: Japan Airlines, declaring bankruptcy, accepted a bailout and agreed to axe 15,600 jobs; Toyota, facing growing criticism about defective accelerator and brake pedals in many of its models, issued a global recall of more than 8.5 million vehicles.

Meanwhile, discontent with the status quo played a major role in Japan's 2008 national elections, when the left-of-center Democratic Party of Japan defeated the conservative Liberal Democratic Party, which had ruled for all but 10 months for the past 50-some years. Under the helm of the new prime minister, Hatoyama Yukio, the DPJ vowed to reshape the Japanese economy by shifting priorities supporting Japan, Inc., to policies focusing on people, including cash handouts to families, support for farmers and fishermen, and tax cuts.

Language

Without a doubt, the hardest part of traveling in Japan is the language barrier. Suddenly you find yourself transported to a crowded land of 127 million people where you can neither speak nor read the language. To make matters worse, many Japanese cannot speak English. And outside big cities and major tourist sites, menus, signs at train stations, and shop names are often in Japanese only.

However, millions of foreign visitors before you who didn't speak a word of Japanese have traveled throughout Japan on their own with great success. Much of the anxiety travelers experience elsewhere is eliminated in Japan because the country is safe and the people are kind and helpful to foreigners. In addition, the country has done a mammoth job during the past decade updating street signs, subway directions, and addresses in Roman letters, especially in Tokyo, Osaka, Kyoto, and other destinations popular with tourists. There are local tourist information offices, called *kanko annaijo,* in almost all cities and towns, usually at train stations. While not all staff speak English, they can provide maps, point out directions, and help with hotel reservations.

In addition, the Japan National Tourist Organization (JNTO) does a super job publishing helpful brochures, leaflets, and maps, including a nifty booklet called *The Tourist's Language Handbook.* It contains sentences in English and their Japanese equivalents for almost every activity, from asking directions, to shopping, to ordering in a restaurant, to staying in a Japanese inn. Pick up a copy at a Tourist Information Center in Tokyo or at Narita or Kansai airports. For more in-depth coverage, there are many language books geared toward travelers, including *Japanese for Travelers* by Scott Rutherford (Tuttle, 2009), with useful phrases and travel tips. It also doesn't hurt to be armed with a small pocket dictionary.

If you need to ask directions of strangers in Japan, your best bet is to ask younger people. They have all studied English in school and are most likely to be able to help you. Japanese businessmen also often know some English. And as strange as it sounds, if you're having problems communicating with someone, write it down so he or she can read it. The emphasis in schools is on written rather than oral English (many English teachers can't speak English themselves), so Japanese who can't understand a word you say may know all the subtleties of syntax and English grammar. If you still have problems communicating, you can always call the Tourist Information Center(tel. 03/3201-3331) to help with translation.

If you're heading out for a particular restaurant, shop, or sight, have your destination written down in Japanese by someone at your hotel. If you get lost along the way, look for one of the police boxes, called *koban,* found in virtually every neighborhood. They have maps of particular districts and can pinpoint exactly where you want to go if you have the address with you.

The Written Language No one knows the exact origins of the Japanese language, but we do know it existed only in spoken form until the 6th century. That's when the Japanese borrowed the Chinese pictorial characters, called *kanji,* and used them to develop their own form of written language. Later, two phonetic alphabet systems, *hiragana* and *katakana,* were added to kanji to form the existing Japanese writing system. Thus, Chinese and Japanese use some of the same pictographs, but otherwise there's no similarity between the languages; while they may be able to recognize parts of each other's written language, the Chinese and Japanese cannot communicate verbally.

The Japanese written language a combination of kanji, hiragana, and katakana is probably one of the most difficult in the modern world. As for the spoken language, there are many levels of speech and forms of expression relating to a person's social status and sex. Even nonverbal communication is a vital part of understanding Japanese, because what isn't said is often more important than what is. It's little wonder that St. Francis Xavier, a Jesuit missionary who came to Japan in the 16th century, wrote that Japanese was an invention of the devil designed to thwart the spread of Christianity. And yet, astoundingly, adult literacy in Japan is estimated to be 99%.

A note on establishment names: Many hotels and restaurants in Japan now have signs in *romaji* (Roman, or English-language, characters) in addition to their Japanese-character signs.

Other Helpful Tips It's worth noting that Japanese nouns do not have plural forms; thus, for example, *ryokan,* a Japanese-style inn, can be both singular and plural, as can kimono. Plural sense is indicated by context.

In addition, the Japanese custom is to list the family name first followed by the given name. That is the format I have followed in this book (with the exception of a few celebrities known outside of Japan), but note that many things printed in English business cards, city brochures, and so on increasingly follow the Western custom of listing the family name last.

And finally, you may find yourself confused because of suffixes attached to Japanese place names. For example, *dori* can mean street, avenue, or road; and sometimes it's attached to a street name with a hyphen, while at other times it stands alone. Thus, you may see Chuo-dori, Chuo Dori, or even Chuo-dori Avenue on English-language maps and street signs, but they're all one and the same street. Likewise, *dera* means "temple" and is often included at the end of the name, as in Kiyomizudera, which may be translated into English as Kiyomizu Temple; *jo* means "castle" and may appear at the end of a castle's name, as in Nijojo, or it may be left off and appear as Nijo Castle.

Written English in Japan English-language words are quite fashionable in Japanese advertising, with the result that you'll often see them on shop signs, posters, shopping bags, and T-shirts. However, the words are often wonderfully misspelled or are used in such unusual contexts that you can only guess at the original intent. What, for example, can possibly be the meaning behind TODAY BIRDS, TOMORROW MEN, which appeared beneath a picture of birds on a shopping bag? I have treasured ashtrays that read THE YOUNG BOY GRASPED HER HEART FIRMLY and LET'S TRIP IN HOKKAIDO. In Okayama, I saw a shop whose name was a stern admonition to customers to GROW UP, while in Gifu you can only surmise at the pleasures to be had at HOTEL JOYBOX.

A staff member of the Hokkaido Tourist Association whose business card identified him working for the PROPAGANDA SECTION was probably more truthful than most. And imagine my consternation upon stepping onto a bathroom scale that called itself the BEAUTY-CHECKER. But the best sign I've seen was at Narita Airport, where each check-in counter displayed a notice advising passengers they would have to pay a service-facility charge at THE TIME OF CHECK-IN FOR YOUR FRIGHT. I explained the cause of my amusement to the person behind the counter, and when I came back 2 weeks later, I was almost disappointed to find that all signs had been corrected. That's Japanese efficiency.

Books, Films & Music

Japanese publisher Kodansha International (www.kodansha-intl.com) has probably published more books on Japan in English including Japanese-language textbooks than any other company. Available at major bookstores in Japan, they are also available at www.amazon.com.

History The definitive work of Japan's history through the ages is *Japan: The Story of a Nation* (Alfred A. Knopf, 1991) by Edwin O. Reischauer, a former U.S. ambassador to Japan. Ivan Morris's *The World of the Shining Prince: Court Life in Ancient Japan* (Kodansha Globe, 1994) highlights the golden age of the imperial court through diaries and literature of the Heian Period (794-1192), while *Everyday Life in Traditional Japan* (Tuttle, 2000) details the daily lives of samurai, farmers, craftsmen, merchants, courtiers, and outcasts during the Edo Period.

For personal accounts of Japan in ages past, there's no better anthology than Donald Keene's *Travelers of a Hundred Ages: The Japanese as Revealed Through 1,000 Years of Diaries* (Holt, 1989). Written by Japanese from all walks of life, the journals provide fascinating insight into the hidden worlds of imperial courts, Buddhist monasteries, isolated country inns, and more. Lafcadio Hearn, a prolific writer about things Japanese, describes life in Japan around the turn of the 20th century in *Writings from Japan* (Penguin, 1985), while Isabella Bird, an Englishwoman who traveled in Japan in the 1870s, writes a vivid account of rural Japanese life in *Unbeaten Tracks in Japan*(Cornell University Library, 2009). *Autobiography of a Geisha* (Columbia University Press, 2003), first published in 1957, is Masuda Sayo's account of being sold to a geisha house as a child, working at a hot-spring spa, and living under harsh conditions during and after World War II.

Society Reischauer's *The Japanese Today: Change and Continuity* (Belknap Press, 1995) offers a unique perspective on the historical events that have shaped and influenced Japanese behavior and the role of the individual in Japanese society. A classic description of Japanese and their culture is found in Ruth Benedict's brilliant *The Chrysanthemum and the Sword: Patterns of Japanese Culture* (Mariner Books, 2006), first published in the 1940s but reprinted many times since. Debunking theories that have long shaped the outside world's views of Japan (many of which are espoused by the books abovex) is *Japan: A Reinterpretation* (Pantheon, 1997) by former *International Herald Tribune* Tokyo bureau chief Patrick Smith, who gives a spirited reinterpretation of Japan's economic miracle and demise; and Alex Kerr's *Dogs and Demons: Tales From the Dark Side of Modern Japan* (Hill and Wang, 2001), who writes a scathing, controversial indictment of a country he loves but says was ruined by corrupt bureaucracy. Jake Adelstein, a former Tokyo crime reporter, writes a gripping account of his run-in with Japanese mafia and the threat on his life in *Tokyo Vice: An American Reporter on the Police Beat in Japan* (Pantheon, 2009).

A more entertaining look at the Japanese psyche is provided by English translations of Japanese articles that never made it into the *Japan Times* in *Tabloid Tokyo: 101 Tales of Sex, Crime, and the Bizarre from Japan's Wild Weeklies* (Kodansha, 2005), edited by Mark Schreiber, and its sequel, *Tabloid Tokyo 2* (Kodansha, 2007).

Culture & the Arts For a cultural overview in one book, see *Introduction to Japanese Culture,* edited by Daniel Sosnoski (Tuttle, 1996), which covers major festivals, the tea ceremony, flower arranging, kabuki, sumo, Japanese board games, Buddhism, kanji, and much more. Elizabeth Kiritani's *Vanishing Japan: Traditions, Crafts & Culture* (Tuttle, 1995) covers a wide spectrum of traditional Japanese crafts and professions that were once a part of daily life, from potato vendors, shoe shiners, and *tatami* makers to Japanese umbrellas and handmade paper, many of which are fast disappearing in today's Japan.

The Japan Travel Bureau puts out nifty pocket-size illustrated booklets on things Japanese, including *A Look into Japan, Living Japanese Style,*

Eating in Japan, Festivals of Japan, and *Japanese Family & Culture,* which covers everything from marriage in Japan to problems with mothers-in-law and explanations of why Dad gets home so late. My favorite is *Salaryman in Japan* (JTB, 1987), which describes the private and working lives of Japan's army of white-collar workers who receive set salaries.

And while some might argue it's not art, there's no denying the power *manga* (Japanese comics) has over Japanese readers. The best primers on manga history and its various genres are Paul Gravett's *Manga: 60 Years of Japanese Comics* (Collins Design, 2004) and, though dated, Frederik L. Schodt and Tezuka Osamu's *Manga! Manga!: The World of Japanese Comics* (Kodansha, 1988), with a follow-up provided in Schodt's *Dreamland Japan: Writings on Modern Manga* (Stone Bridge Press, 1996). Likewise, travelers new to Japanese animation should check out *Anime from Akira to Howl's Moving Castle* by Susan J. Napier (Palgrave Macmillan, 2005).

Contemporary Chronicles For contemporary experiences of foreigners in Japan, there's the inimitable Dave Barry, who describes his whirlwind trip to the Land of the Rising Sun in the comical *Dave Barry Does Japan* (Random House, 1992) and solves such puzzling mysteries as why Japanese cars sell successfully (they're made of steel!). A delightful account of Japanese and their customs is given by the irrepressible George Mikes in *The Land of the Rising Yen* (Penguin, 1973). *Traveler's Tales Guides: Japan*(Traveler's Tales, 1999) relates the firsthand experiences of Dave Barry, Pico Iyer, and other writers who tackle such issues as sand bathing and Washlet toilets. A book seemingly from another era is *Geisha* (Vintage, 2000) by Liza C. Dalby, which describes her year living as a geisha in Kyoto as part of a research project. *The Japan Journals: 1947-2004* (Stone Bridge Press, 2004) by film scholar Donald Richie provides personal insight to Japan's transformation from a postwar nation to a cultural and economic powerhouse.

Fiction Whenever I travel in Japan, I especially enjoy reading fictional accounts of the country; they help put me in tune with my surroundings and increase my awareness and perception. The world's first major novel was written by a Japanese woman, Murasaki Shikibu, whose classic, *The Tale of Genji* (Knopf, 1978), dating from the 11th century, describes the aristocratic life of Prince Genji.

Tokyo bookstores have entire sections dedicated to English-language translations of Japan's best-known modern and contemporary authors, including Mishima Yukio, Soseki Natsume, Abe Kobo, Tanizaki Junichiro, and Nobel Prize winners Kawabata Yasunari and Oe

Kenzaburo. An overview of Japanese classical literature from the earliest times to the mid-19th century is provided in *Anthology of Japanese Literature*(Grove Press, 1988), edited by Donald Keene. Likewise, *The Showa Anthology: Modern Japanese Short Stories* (Kodansha, 1992), edited by Van C. Gessel and Tomone Matsumoto, covers works by Abe Kobe, Mishima Yukio, Kawabata Yasunari, Oe Kenzaburo, and others written between 1929 and 1984, while *Modern Japanese Stories: An Anthology* (Tuttle, 1962), edited by Ivan Morris, introduces short stories by some of Japan's top modern writers, including Mori Ogai, Tanizaki Junichiro, Kawabata Yasunari, and Mishima Yukio.

For novels, you might read Mishima's *The Sea of Fertility* (Knopf), a collection of four separate works, the last of which, *The Decay of the Angel,* was delivered to his publisher on the day of his suicide; or *The Sound of Waves* (Knopf, 1956), about young love in a Japanese fishing village. Other famous works by Japanese authors include Soseki Natsume's first novel, *I am a Cat* (Tuttle, 1972), which describes the foibles of upper-middle-class Japanese during the Meiji Era through the eyes of a cat; and his later novel, *Kokoro* (Regnery Gateway Co., 1985), as well as Kawabata Yasunari's *Snow Country* (Knopf, 1956), translated by Edward G. Seidensticker. Although not well known in the West, Enchi Fumiko wrote an absorbing novel about women in an upper-class, late-19th-century family in *The Waiting Years* (Kodansha, 2002), first published in 1957. Tanizaki Junichiro's *Makioka Sisters* (Vintage, 1995) is an epic tale of four Japanese sisters during the turbulent 1940s and 1950s.

Oe Kenzaburo gained international recognition when he became the second Japanese to win the Nobel Prize for literature in 1994. One of his best-known novels is *Nip the Buds, Shoot the Kids* (Grove Press, 1996), a disturbing tale of a group of reform-school boys in the waning days of World War II. *A Personal Matter* (Grove Press, 1968) is about a man in search of himself after the birth of a handicapped son. *Hiroshima Notes*(Grove/Atlantic, 1996), featuring personal accounts of atomic bomb survivors, is a moving commentary on the meaning of the Hiroshima bombing.

Favorite writers of Japan's baby-boom generation include Murakami Ryu, who burst onto the literary scene with *Almost Transparent Blue* (Kodansha, 1977), and later captured the undercurrent of decadent urban life in his best-selling *Coin Locker Babies*(Kodansha, 1995). He wrote a shocking exposé of Tokyo's sex industry, *In the Miso Soup* (Kodansha, 2003). Murakami Haruki's writings include *Dance Dance Dance*(Kodansha, 1994); *Hard-Boiled Wonderland and the End of the World* (Vintage, 1993); *The Wind-Up Bird Chronicle* (Knopf, 1997);

South of the Border, West of the Sun (Knopf, 1999); and *Norwegian Wood* (Vintage, 2000), a coming-of-age story set during the 1969 student movement in Japan. His *After the Quake: Stories* (Knopf, 2002) centers on fictional characters in the months after the 1995 Kobe earthquake.

For works of fiction about Japan by Western writers, most Westerners are familiar with James Clavell's *Shogun* (Dell, 1975), a fictional account based on the lives of Englishman William Adams and military leader Tokugawa Ieyasu around 1600. The best-selling *Memoirs of a Geisha* (Knopf, 1997), by Arthur Golden and also a movie, is the fictional autobiography of a fisherman's daughter sold to a geisha house, later becoming one of Kyoto's most celebrated geisha of the 1930s.

For fictional yet personal contemporary accounts of what it's like for Westerners living in Japan, entertaining novels include *Ransom* (Vintage, 1985) by Jay McInerney and *Pictures from the Water Trade* (Harper & Row, 1986) by John D. Morley. Pico Iyer taps into the mysterious juxtaposition of the old Japan vs. the new in *The Lady and the Monk: Four Seasons in Kyoto* (Knopf, 1991). *Audrey Hepburn's Neck* (Simon & Schuster, 1996) is Alan Brown's poignant portrait of Japan's mishmash of Western and Japanese culture, as seen through the eyes of a confused young Japanese comic illustrator. Mystery fans should read Sujata Massey's 10 novels following the adventures of Japanese-American Rei Shimura; her *Girl in a Box* (HarperCollins, 2006), follows Rei's cross-cultural escapades as she works undercover in a Japanese department store.

Films

The classic samurai film is probably Kurosawa Akira's *The Seven Samurai* (1954), remade into the western *The Magnificent Seven*. Other films by what some consider to be Japan's greatest filmmaker include *Rashomon* (1951), about a murder and a rape and that raises as many questions as it answers about human nature; *Kagemusha* (1980), about warlords battling for control at the end of feudal Japan; and *Ran* (1985), an epic drama set in 16th-century Japan and based on Shakespeare's *King Lear*. For a look at Japan's mountain people in the 1880s, nothing can beat Kinoshita Keisuke's *Ballad of Narayama* (1958), with its unsentimental portrait of an elderly woman who goes off into the snowy countryside to die, as was the custom of her people.

Director Oshima Nagisa created a stir in the film world with *In the Realm of the Senses* (1976), a story of obsessive love so graphic and erotic it remains censored in Japan. Juzo Itami, a famous Japanese director who purportedly leapt to his death in Tokyo in 1997 (the circumstances are mysterious), is remembered for his humorous satires on Japanese life, including *Tampopo* (1985), about sex and food and a Japanese woman who achieves success with a noodle shop; *The Funeral* (1984), which takes a comic look at death in Japan, including the surviving family's helplessness when it comes to arranging the complex rituals of the Buddhist ceremony; and *A Taxing Woman* (1987), about a female tax auditor.

Love and Pop (1998), by director Anno Hideaki, best known for *anime* films, is a low-budget film based on a novel by Murakami Ryu about "compensated dating," in which teenage girls are paid to go out with older businessmen. Another film dealing with this phenomenon rarely covered in the Western press is Harada Masato's *Bounce Ko Gals*(1998), which presents a shocking but heartfelt story of sexual exploitation and loss of innocence.

A commentary on Japan's economic woes on a personal level is *Tokyo Sonata* (2008), directed Kurosawa Kiyoshi, about a father who loses his job but is too ashamed to tell his family and thus pretends he's going to work every day. *Departures* (2008) is Takita Yojiro's moving Academy Award-winning film (for best foreign film) about a musician who takes a job preparing corpses and eventually comes to see it as a deeply rewarding profession.

Probably the most internationally well-known film shot in Tokyo in recent years is Sophia Coppola's *Lost in Translation* (2003), in which two lost characters take solace in each other's company as they drift through an incomprehensible and at times hilarious Tokyo, while *The Harimaya Bridge* (2009), by Aaron Woolfolk, is a moving story about a man whose hatred for Japanese (his father died in a Japanese POW camp) slowly dissolves when he travels to Kochi to pick up his dead son's belongings.

One of Japan's most famous animated films is Miyazaki Hayao's *Spirited Away* (2001), about a young girl who must call upon her inner strength to save herself and her family.

Religion

The main religions in Japan are Shintoism and Buddhism, and many Japanese consider themselves believers in both. Most Japanese, for example, will marry in a Shinto ceremony, but when they die, they'll have a Buddhist funeral.

A native religion of Japan, **Shintoism** is the worship of ancestors and national heroes, as well as of all natural things, both animate and inanimate. These natural things are thought to embody gods and can be anyone or anything mountains, trees, the moon, stars, rivers, seas, fires, rocks, and animals. Shintoism also embraces much of Confucianism, which entered Japan in the 5th century and stressed the importance of family and loyalty. There are no scriptures in Shintoism, nor any ordained code of morals or ethics.

The place of worship in Shintoism is called a *jinja,* or shrine. The most obvious sign of a shrine is its *torii,* an entrance gate, usually of wood, consisting of two tall poles topped with either one or two crossbeams. Another feature common to shrines is a water trough with communal cups, where the Japanese will wash their hands and sometimes rinse out their mouths. Purification and cleanliness are important in Shintoism because they show respect to the gods. At the shrine, worshipers will throw a few coins into a money box, clap their hands twice to get the gods' attention, and then bow their heads and pray for whatever they wish good health, protection, the safe delivery of a child, or a prosperous year.

Founded in India in the 6th to 5th centuries B.C., Buddhism came to Japan in the 6th century A.D. via China and Korea, bringing with it the concept of eternal life. By the end of the 6th century, Buddhism had gained such popularity that the prince regent Shotoku, one of Japan's most remarkable historical figures, declared Buddhism the state religion and based many of his governmental policies on its tenets. Another important Buddhist leader to emerge was a priest called Kukai, known posthumously as Kobo Daishi. After studying Buddhism in China in the early 800s, he returned and built temples throughout Japan, including the famous 88 temples on Shikoku island and those on Mount Koya, which continue to attract millions of pilgrims today.

Of the various Buddhist sects in Japan today, Zen Buddhism is probably the most well known in the West. Considered the most Japanese form of Buddhism, Zen is the practice of meditation and a strictly disciplined lifestyle to rid yourself of desire so that you can achieve enlightenment. There are no rites in Zen Buddhism, no dogmas, no theological conceptions of divinity. You do not analyze rationally, but rather know things intuitively. The strict and simple lifestyle of Zen appealed greatly to Japan's samurai warrior class, and many of Japan's arts, including the tea ceremony, arose from the practice of Zen.

Whereas Shintoists have shrines, Buddhists have temples, called *otera*. Instead of torii, temples will often have an entrance gate with a raised doorsill and heavy doors. Temples may also have a cemetery on their grounds (which Shinto shrines never have) as well as a pagoda.

Travel and Tourism
Planning a Trip to Japan

From experience, I know that the two biggest concerns for visitors to Japan are the language barrier and the high cost of living. To help alleviate fears about the first, I've provided a glossary of useful words and phrases, given the Japanese characters for establishments that do not have English-language signs so you can recognize their names, outlined tips for dealing with the language barrier, given brief instructions on how to reach most of the places I recommend, made suggestions for ordering in restaurants without English-language menus, and provided prices for everything from subway rides to admission to museums.

As for costs, probably everyone has heard horror stories about Japan's high prices. Ever since the dramatic fall of the dollar against the yen in the 1980s and 1990s, Tokyo and Osaka have been two of the world's most expensive cities, with food and lodging costing as much as in

New York or London, maybe more. But after Japan's economic bubble burst in the early 1990s, something happened that would have been unthinkable during the heady spending days of the 1980s: Japanese became bargain conscious. There are now inexpensive French bistros, secondhand clothing stores, 100-yen shops, and budget hotels.

Still, it's difficult not to suffer an initial shock from Japan's high prices, which will seem especially exorbitant if you insist on living and eating exactly as you do back home. The secret is to live and eat as Japanese do. This book will help you do exactly that, with descriptions of eateries and Japanese-style inns that cater to the native population. By following this book's advice and exercising a little caution on your own, you should be able to cut down on needless expenses and learn even more about Japan in the process. While you may never find Japan cheap, you will find it richly rewarding for all the reasons you chose Japan as a destination in the first place.

Despite the difficulties inherent in visiting any foreign country, I think you'll find Japan very easy to navigate. There are many more signs in English now than there were even just a decade ago. And Japan remains one of the safest countries in the world; in general, you don't have to worry about muggers, pickpockets, or crooks. In fact, I sometimes feel downright coddled in Japan. Everything runs like clockwork: Trains are on time, public telephones work, and the service whether in hotels, restaurants, or department stores ranks among the best in the world. I know if I get truly lost, someone will help me and will probably even go out of his or her way to do so. Japanese are honest and extremely helpful toward foreign visitors. Indeed, it's the people themselves who make traveling in Japan such a delight.

This section will help you with the what, when, where, and how of travel to Japan from what documents you need (only passports for most nationalities) to how to get around easily and economically (you'll want to purchase a Japan Rail Pass *before* going to Japan).

Health & Insurance

Staying Healthy

It's safe to drink tap water and eat to your heart's content everywhere in Japan (pregnant women, however, are advised to avoid eating raw fish or taking hot baths). Although Japan had nine cases of mad cow disease after its first confirmed case in 2001, all slaughtered cows must now be checked for the disease before the meat is authorized for consumption. To prevent the spread of avian and H1N1 flu, all incoming passengers are monitored upon arrival at Narita Airport for fever; those with a higher than normal temperature may be quarantined. To be on the safe side, therefore, you may opt for an influenza vaccine before departing from home.

Otherwise, you don't need any inoculations to enter Japan. Note: Prescriptions can be filled at Japanese pharmacies only if they're issued by a Japanese doctor. To avoid hassle, bring more prescription medications than you think you'll need, clearly labeled in their original vials, and be sure to pack them in your carry-on luggage. But to be safe, bring copies of your prescriptions with you, including generic names of medicines in case a local pharmacist is unfamiliar with the brand name. Over-the-counter items are easy to obtain, though name brands are likely to be different from back home, some ingredients allowed elsewhere may be forbidden in Japan, and prices are likely to be higher.

What to Do If You Get Sick Away from Home If you get sick, contact the concierge at your hotel some upper-range hotels, especially in Tokyo, have in-house doctors or clinics. Otherwise, your concierge, consulate, and sometimes even the local tourist office can provide a list of area doctors who speak English. You can also contact the International Association for Medical Assistance to Travellers (tel. 716/754-4883, or 416/652-0137 in Canada; www.iamat.org), an organization that lists many local English-speaking doctors and also posts the latest developments in global outbreaks. Otherwise, if you can't find a doctor who can help you right away, try the local hospital. Many have walk-in-clinics for cases that are not life-threatening. Doctors and hospitals generally do not accept credit cards and require immediate cash payment for health services.

Healthy Travels to You

The following government websites offer up-to-date health-related travel advice.

- Australia: www.smartraveller.gov.au/tips/travelwell.html
- Canada: www.hc-sc.gc.ca/index-eng.php
- U.K.: www.nhs.uk/healthcareabroad/pages/healthcareabroad.aspx
- U.S.: www.cdc.gov/travel

Safety

One of the greatest delights of traveling in Japan is that the country is safe and the people are honest. When a friend of mine forgot her purse in a public restroom in Osaka, someone turned it in to the police station complete with money, digital camera, and passport. In all the years I've lived and worked in Japan, I've never had even one fearful encounter, and I never hesitate to walk anywhere any time of the night or day. If you lose something, say on a subway or in a park, chances are good that you'll get it back.

That being said, crime especially pickpocketing is on the increase, and there are precautions you should always take when traveling: Stay alert and be aware of your immediate surroundings. Be especially careful with cameras, purses, and wallets in congested areas like Narita airport, subways, department stores, or tourist attractions (like the retail district around Tokyo's Tsukiji Market). Some Japanese caution women against walking through parks alone at night.

Money

Currency conversions can fluctuate widely; if I could advise you accurately on the future exchange rate, I'd be too rich to be a guidebook writer. Consult a currency-exchange website such as www.xe.com to check up-to-the-minute rates.

Currency The currency in Japan is called the *yen,* symbolized by ¥. Coins come in denominations of ¥1, ¥5, ¥10, ¥50, ¥100, and ¥500. Bills come in denominations of ¥1,000, ¥2,000, ¥5,000, and ¥10,000, though ¥2,000 notes are rarely seen. You'll find that all coins get used (though it's hard to get rid of ¥1 coins). Keep plenty of change handy for riding local transportation such as buses or streetcars. Although change machines are virtually everywhere, even on buses where you can change larger coins and ¥1,000 bills, you'll find it faster to have the exact amount on hand.

Some people like to arrive in a foreign country with that country's currency already on hand, but I do not find it necessary for Japan. Narita, Kansai, and Nagoya international airports all have exchange counters for all incoming international flights that offer better exchange rates than what you'd get abroad, as well as ATMs. I usually change enough money to last several days.

Personal checks are not used in Japan. Most Japanese pay with either credit cards or cash and because the country overall has such a low crime rate, you can feel safe walking around with money (though of course you should always exercise caution). The only time you really need to be alert to possible pickpockets in Japan is when you're riding a crowded subway during rush hour or walking in heavily visited areas of Tokyo and other large cities.

In any case, although the bulk of your expenses hotels, train tickets, major purchases, meals in tourist-oriented restaurants can be paid for with credit cards, you'll want to bring traveler's checks for those times when you might not have easy access to an ATM for cash withdrawals.

ATMs The best way to get cash away from home is from an ATM (automated teller machine). Because most bank ATMs in Japan accept only cards issued by Japanese banks, your best bet for obtaining cash is at 7-Eleven convenience stores, which are found throughout Japan, are often open 24 hours, and have ATMs that accept foreign bank cards operating on the Cirrus (www.mastercard.com) and PLUS (www.visa.com) systems, as well as American Express.

Another good bet is at one of 21,000 post offices, which also have ATMs accepting foreign bank cards operating on the Cirrus and PLUS systems. Although major post offices, usually located near main train stations, have long open hours for ATMs (generally 7am-11pm weekdays and 9am-7 or 9pm on weekends), small post offices may have only limited hours for ATMs (depending on the post office, that may be until 6 or 7pm weekdays and until 5pm on weekends).

Other places with ATMs that might accept foreign-issued cards include Citibank and large department stores in major cities. Note that there is no public American Express office in Japan.

Be sure you know your four-digit personal identification number (PIN) and your daily withdrawal limit before leaving home. Also keep in mind that many banks impose a fee every time a card is used at a different bank's ATM, and that fee can be higher for international transactions than for domestic ones. In addition, the bank from which you withdraw cash may charge its own fee. For international withdrawal fees, ask your bank.

Credit Cards Credit cards are a safe way to carry money, provide a convenient record of all your expenses, and generally offer relatively good exchange rates. You can withdraw cash advances from your credit cards at banks or ATMs, provided you know your four-digit PIN. Keep in mind that you'll pay interest from the moment of your withdrawal, even if you pay your monthly bills on time. Also, note that many banks assess a 1% to 3% "transaction fee" on all charges you incur abroad (whether you're using the local currency or your native currency).

The most readily accepted cards are MasterCard (also called Eurocard), Visa, and the Japanese credit card JCB (Japan Credit Bank); many tourist-oriented facilities also accept American Express and Diners Club. Shops and restaurants accepting credit and charge cards will usually post which cards they accept at the door or near the cash register. However, some establishments may be reluctant to accept cards for small purchases and inexpensive meals, so inquire beforehand. In addition, note that the vast majority of Japan's smaller and least-expensive businesses, including many restaurants, noodle shops, fast-food joints, ma-and-pa establishments, and the cheapest accommodations, do not accept credit cards.

Traveler's Checks While traveler's checks are something of an anachronism now that ATMs have come onto the scene, they're still useful for Japan, where ATMs for foreign-issued cards are limited primarily to 7-Eleven convenience stores and post offices. Traveler's checks fetch a better exchange rate than cash and also offer protection in case of theft (be sure to keep a record of the traveler's checks' serial numbers separate from your checks in the event that they are stolen or lost). Note, however, that in some very remote areas, even banks won't cash them. Before taking off for small towns, therefore, be sure you have enough cash.

Exchanging Money All banks in Japan displaying an AUTHORIZED FOREIGN EXCHANGE sign can exchange currency and traveler's checks, with exchange rates usually displayed at the appropriate foreign-exchange counter. Banks are generally open Monday through Friday from 9am to 3pm, though business hours for exchanging foreign currency usually don't begin until 10:30 or 11am (be prepared for a long wait; you'll be asked to sit down as your order is processed). More convenient and quicker are Travelex (www.travelex.com)

foreign-exchange kiosks, with locations in several cities in Japan, including Tokyo, Kyoto, Nagoya, Osaka, and Sapporo.

If you need to exchange money outside banking hours, inquire at your hotel. Likewise, large department stores also offer exchange services and are often open until 7:30 or 8pm. Note, however, that hotels and department stores may charge a handling fee, offer a slightly less favorable exchange rate, and require a passport for all transactions.

Actualities

American Express: There are no American Express customer-service offices in Japan.

Area Codes: All telephone area codes for Japanese cities begin with a zero (03 for Tokyo, 06 for Osaka, 075 for Kyoto), but drop the first zero if calling Japan from abroad.

Business Hours: Government offices and private companies are generally open Monday through Friday 9am to 5pm. Banks are open Monday through Friday 9am to 3pm (but usually will not exchange money until 10:30 or 11am, after that day's currency exchange rates come in). Neighborhood post offices are open Monday through Friday 9am to 5pm. Major post offices, however (usually located near major train stations), have longer hours and may be open weekends as well.

(Some central post offices, such as those in Tokyo and Osaka, are open 24 hr. for mail.)

Department stores are open from about 10am to 8pm. Most are open daily but may close irregularly (always the same day of the week). Smaller stores are generally open from 10am to 8pm, closed 1 day a week. Convenience stores such as 7-Eleven and Family Mart are open 24 hours.

Keep in mind that museums, gardens, and attractions stop selling admission tickets at least 30 minutes before the actual closing time. Similarly, restaurants take their last orders at least 30 minutes before the posted closing time (even earlier for *kaiseki*restaurants). Most national, prefectural, and city museums are closed on Monday; if Monday is a national holiday, however, they'll remain open and close on the following day, Tuesday, instead. Privately owned museums, however, are usually closed on holidays.

Drinking Laws: The legal drinking age is 20. Beer, wine, and spirits are readily available in grocery stores, some convenience stores, and liquor stores. Many bars, especially in nightlife districts such as Shinjuku and Roppongi, are open until dawn. If you intend to drive in Japan, you are not allowed even one drink.

Drugstores: Drugstores, called *kusuri-ya,* are found readily in Japan. Note, however, that you cannot have a foreign prescription filled in Japan without first consulting a doctor in Japan, so it's best to bring an adequate supply of important medicines with you. No drugstores in Japan stay open 24 hours. However, ubiquitous convenience stores like 7-Eleven, Lawson, and Family Mart, open day and night throughout Japan, carry such nonprescription items as aspirin.

Earthquakes: Kobe's tragic 1995 earthquake brought attention to the fact that Japan is earthquake-prone, but in reality, most earthquakes are too small to detect (of the more than 100,000 earthquakes annually in Japan, only 1% are big enough to feel). However, in case of an earthquake you can feel, there are a few precautions you should take. If you're indoors, take cover under a doorway or against a wall and do not go outdoors. If you're outdoors, stay away from trees, power lines, and the sides of buildings; if you're surrounded by tall buildings, seek cover in a doorway. If you're near a beach or the bay, evacuate to higher ground in case of a tsunami. Never use elevators during a quake. Other precautions include noting emergency exits wherever you stay; all hotels supply flashlights, usually found attached to your bedside table. More information on earthquakes is provided by the Japan Meteorological Agency at www.jma.go.jp.

Electricity: The electricity throughout Japan is 100 volts AC, but there are two different cycles in use: In Tokyo and in regions northeast of the capital, it's 50 cycles, while in Nagoya, Kyoto, Osaka, and all points to the southwest, it's 60 cycles. Leading hotels in Tokyo often have two outlets, one for 100 volts and one for 220 volts; almost all have hair dryers in the rooms. You can use many American appliances in Japan because the American standard is 110 volts and 60 cycles, but they may run a little slowly. Note, too, that the flat, two-legged prongs used in Japan are the same size and fit as in North America, but three-pronged appliances are not accepted.

Embassies & Consulates: Most embassies are located in Tokyo. There are, however, U.S., British, New Zealand, and Australian consulates in Osaka. For the location of other consulates, inquire at the respective embassies.

Emergencies: The national emergency numbers are tel. 110 for police and tel. 119for ambulance and fire (ambulances are free in Japan unless you request a specific hospital). You do not need to insert any money into public telephones to call these numbers. However, if you use a green public telephone, it's necessary to push a red button before dialing. If you call from a gray public telephone or one that accepts only prepaid cards, you won't see a red button; in that case simply lift the receiver and dial. Be sure to speak slowly and precisely.

Language: English is widely understood in major hotels, restaurants, and shops, but it's hit-or-miss elsewhere. Be sure to pick up the free "Tourist's Language Handbook," at the Tourist Information Center.

Laundry & Dry Cleaning: All upper- and most midrange hotels offer laundry and dry-cleaning services (but it's expensive, with a laundered shirt costing about ¥400). For same-day service, it's usually necessary to turn in your laundry by 10am; many hotels do not offer laundry service on Sundays and holidays. Budget accommodations sometimes have coin-operated machines. Otherwise, coin-laundries (as they're known in Japan) are abundant, and many hotel guest rooms have a pullout laundry line over the tub for hand washables.

Legal Aid: Contact your embassy if you find yourself in legal trouble. The Legal Counseling Center, 1-4 Yotsuya, Shinjuku (tel. 03/5367-5280; www.horitsu-sodan.jp; station: Yotsuya), is operated by three bar associations and provides legal counseling with English interpreters Monday to Friday from 1 to 4pm.

Lost & Found: If you've forgotten something on a subway, in a taxi, or on a park bench, don't assume it's gone forever; if you're willing to trace it, you'll probably get it back. If you can remember where you last saw it, the first thing to do is telephone the establishment or return to where you left it, as there's a good chance it will still be sitting there. If you've lost something on the street, go to the nearest *koban* (police box); items found in the neighborhood will stay there for 3 days or longer.

Be sure to notify all your credit card companies the minute you discover your wallet has been lost or stolen. Visa's emergency number in Japan is tel. 00531/11-15555. American Express cardholders can call tel. 03/3220-6220 and for traveler's checks it's tel. 0120/779-656. MasterCard holders should call tel. 00531/11-3886 and Diners Club holders should call tel. 0120/074-024 in Japan.

Luggage & Lockers: Storage space on Shinkansen bullet trains is limited, so travel with the smallest bag you can get away with. Coin-operated lockers are located at major train stations as well as at most subway stations, but most lockers are generally not large enough to store huge pieces of luggage (and those that do are often taken). Lockers generally cost ¥300 to ¥800 depending on the size. Some major stations also have check-in rooms for luggage, though these are rare. If your bag becomes too much to handle, you can have it sent ahead via *takkyu-bin*, an efficient forwarding service available at upper-range hotels and all convenience stores in Japan. At Narita and

Kansai international airports, service counters will send luggage to your hotel the next day (or vice versa) for about ¥2,000 per bag.

Mail: If your hotel cannot mail letters for you, ask the concierge for the location of the nearest post office, recognizable by the red logo of a capital T with a horizontal line over it. Mailboxes are bright orange-red. It costs ¥110 to airmail letters weighing up to 25 grams and ¥70 for postcards to Australia, North America, and Europe. Domestic mail costs ¥80 for letters up to 25 grams, and ¥50 for postcards. Post offices throughout Japan are also convenient for their ATMs, which accept international bank cards operating on the PLUS and Cirrus systems, as well as MasterCard and Visa.

Although all post offices are open Monday through Friday from 9am to 5pm, international post offices (often located close to the central train station) have longer hours, often until 7pm or later on weekdays and with open hours also on weekends (in Tokyo and Osaka, counters are open 24 hr.). If your hotel does not have a shipping service, it is only at these larger post offices that you can mail packages abroad. Conveniently, they sell cardboard boxes in several sizes with the necessary tape. Packages sent via surface mail cannot weigh more than 20 kilograms (about 44 lb.) and take about a month to reach North America, with a package weighing 10 kilograms (about 22 lb.)

costing ¥6,750. Express packages, which take 3 days to North America and can weigh up to 30 kilograms (66 lb.), cost ¥12,550 for 10 kilograms (22 lb.). For more information, visit www.post.japanpost.jp.

Measurements: Before the metric system came into use in Japan, the country had its own standards for measuring length and weight. Rooms are still measured by the number of *tatami* straw mats that will fit in them. A six-tatami room, for example, is the size of six tatami mats, with a tatami roughly .9m (3 ft.) wide and 1.8m (6 ft.) long.

Newspapers & Magazines: Three English-language newspapers are published daily in Japan: the *Japan Times* and the *Daily Yomiuri* (the former with a weekly supplement from *The Observer* and the latter with a weekly supplement from the *Washington Post*), as well as the *International Herald Tribune/Asahi Shimbun*. Major bookstores carry the international editions of such newsmagazines as *Time* and *Newsweek*. You can also read the *Japan Times* online at www.japantimes.co.jp and the *Daily Yomiuri* at www.yomiuri.co.jp/dy.

Police: The national emergency number for police is tel. 110.

Smoking: You must be 20 years old to smoke in Japan. Smoking is banned in most public areas, including train and subway stations and office buildings. In many cities, ordinances also ban smoking on sidewalks but allow it in marked areas, usually near train stations.

Many restaurants have nonsmoking sections, though bars do not. Most hotels have designated nonsmoking floors nowadays, though Japanese-style inns, because of their small size, usually do not; some business hotels also don't. If you want to sit in the nonsmoking car of the Shinkansen bullet train, ask for the *kinensha* (some lines are completely smoke-free); during peak times, be sure to reserve a seat in the nonsmoking car in advance.

Taxes: A 5% consumption tax is imposed on goods and services in Japan, including hotel rates and restaurant meals. Although hotels and restaurants are required to include the tax in their published rates, a few have yet to comply (especially on English-language menus). In Tokyo, hotels also levy a separate accommodations tax of ¥100 to ¥200 per person per night. In hot-spring resort areas, a ¥150 *onsen* tax is added for every night of your stay.

In addition to these taxes, a 10% to 15% service charge will be added to your bill in lieu of tipping at most of the fancier restaurants and at moderately priced and upper-end hotels; in *ryokan,* service charge can be as high as 20%. Business hotels, *minshuku,* youth hostels, and inexpensive restaurants do not impose a service charge.

As for shopping, a 5% consumption tax is also included in the price of most goods. (Some of the smaller vendors are not required to levy tax.) Travelers from abroad, however, are eligible for an exemption on goods taken out of the country, although only the larger department stores and specialty shops seem equipped to deal with the procedures. In any case, most department stores grant a refund on the consumption tax only when the total amount of purchases for the day at their store exceeds ¥10,000. You can obtain a refund immediately by having a sales clerk fill out a list of your purchases and then presenting the list to the tax-exemption counter of the department store; *you will need to show your passport.* Note that no refunds for consumption tax are given for food, drinks, tobacco, cosmetics, film, and batteries.

Television: If you enjoy watching television, you've come to the wrong country. Almost nothing is broadcast in English; even foreign films are dubbed in Japanese. Most upper-range hotels, however, offer bilingual televisions, whereby you can switch from Japanese to English if the program or movie was originally in English, though only a few (and fairly dated) English movies and sitcoms are broadcast each week. The plus of bilingual TVs is that you can listen to the nightly national news broadcast by NHK at 7 and 9pm. Otherwise, major hotels in larger cities have cable or satellite TV with English-language programs including CNN broadcasts (sometimes in Japanese only) and BBC World as well as in-house pay movies. But even if you don't understand Japanese, I suggest that you watch TV at least once; maybe you'll catch a samurai series or a sumo match. Commercials are also worth watching. *Note:* Japan switches from analog to digital broadcasting in July 2011. Many hotels have already replaced older TV sets with new equipment.

A word on those pay video programs offered by hotels and many resort *ryokan:*Upper-range hotels usually have a few choices in English, and these are charged automatically to your bill. Most business hotels, however, usually offer only one kind of pay movie generally "adult entertainment." If you're traveling with children, you'll want to be extremely careful about selecting your TV programs. Many adult video pay channels appear with a simple push of the channel-selector button, and they can be difficult to get rid of. In budget accommodations, you may come across televisions with coin boxes attached to their sides, or, more common nowadays, vending machines offering prepaid cards. These are also for special adult entertainment videos. Now you know.

Time: Japan is 9 hours ahead of Greenwich Mean Time, 14 hours ahead of New York, 15 hours ahead of Chicago, and 17 hours ahead of Los Angeles. Because Japan does not go on daylight saving time, subtract 1 hour from the above times in the summer when calling from countries that have daylight saving time such as the United States.

Because Japan is on the other side of the international date line, you lose a day when traveling from the United States to Asia. (If you depart the United States on Tues, you'll arrive on Wed.) Returning to North America, however, you gain a day, which means that you arrive on the same day you left. (In fact, it can happen that you arrive in the States at an earlier hour than you departed from Japan.)

Tipping: One of the delights of being in Japan is that there's no tipping not even to waitresses, taxi drivers, or bellhops. If you try to tip them, they'll probably be confused or embarrassed. Instead, you'll have a 10% to 15% service charge added to your bill at higher-priced accommodations and restaurants. That being said, you might want to tip, say, your room attendant at a high-class *ryokan* if you've made special requests or meals are served in your room; in that case, place crisp, clean bills (¥3,000-¥5,000) in a white envelope on the table of your room at the beginning of your stay; but it's perfectly fine if you choose not to tip.

Toilets: If you need a restroom, your best bets are at train and subway stations (though these can be dirty), big hotels, department stores, and fast-food restaurants. Use of restrooms is free in Japan, and though many public facilities supply toilet paper, it's a good idea to carry a packet of tissues, because many others do not.

In parks and some restaurants, especially in rural areas, don't be surprised if you go into some restrooms and find men's urinals and private stalls in the same room. Women are supposed to walk right past the urinals without noticing them.

Many toilets in Japan, especially those at train stations, are Japanese-style toilets: They're holes in the ground over which you squat facing forward toward the end with a raised hood. Men stand and aim for the hole. Although Japanese lavatories may seem uncomfortable at first, they're actually more sanitary because no part of your body touches anything.

Western-style toilets in Japan are usually very high-tech. Called Washlets, these combination bidet toilets have heated toilet seats, buttons and knobs directing sprays of water of various intensities to various body parts, and even lids that raise when you open the stall. But alas, instructions are usually in Japanese only. Listen to the voice of experience: Don't stand up until you've figured out how to turn the darn spray off.

Water: The water is safe to drink anywhere in Japan, although some people claim it's too highly chlorinated. Bottled water is also readily available.

Weather: Everything from daily forecasts to estimated dates for the cherry blossom or rainy season, along with other fun data, is available from the Japan Meteorological Agency at www.jma.go.jp.

Visitor Information

The Japan National Tourist Organization (JNTO) publishes a wealth of free, colorful brochures and maps. Be sure to get "The Tourist's Language Handbook," a phrase booklet to help foreign visitors communicate with Japanese. Other useful JNTO publications include the free "Tourist Map of Japan," showing the four major islands and major highway and railway lines, with maps of major cities on the reverse side; a "Directory of Welcome Inns," which lists inexpensive accommodations throughout Japan, with a free reservation system; and the invaluable "Railway Timetable," which contains timetables for Shinkansen trains and major train lines throughout Japan.

JNTO Online: You can reach JNTO via the Internet at www.jnto.go.jp (and at www.japantravelinfo.com for North American travelers; www.seejapan.co.ukfor British travelers; and www.jnto.org.au for

Australian travelers), where you can read up on what's new, view maps, get the latest weather report, find links to online hotel reservation companies and tour companies, and browse through information ranging from hints on budget travel to regional events. JNTO also showcases local's tourism attractions, Japanese cuisine, and other topics on YouTube at www.youtube.com/visitjapan.

JNTO Overseas: If you'd like information on Japan before leaving home, contact one of the following JNTO offices:

In the United States: 11 W. 42nd St., 19th floor, New York, NY 10036 (tel. 212/757-5640; visitjapan@jntonyc.org); and Little Tokyo Plaza 340 E. 2nd St., Ste. 302, Los Angeles, CA 90012 (tel. 213/623-1952; info@jnto-lax.org).

In Canada: 481 University Ave., Ste. 306, Toronto, ON M5G 2E9, Canada (tel. 416/366-7140; info@jntoyyz.com).

In the United Kingdom: Fifth Floor, 12 Nicholas Lane, London EC4N 7BN, England (tel. 020/7398-5678; info@jnto.co.uk).

In Australia: Level 7, 36-38 Clarence St., Sydney NSW 2000, Australia (no phone; travelinfo@jnto.org.au).

JNTO in Japan: Your best bet for general or specific information on Japan is at one of JNTO's three excellent Tourist Information Centers

(TICs). They're located in downtown Tokyo, at Narita Airport outside Tokyo, and at Kansai International Airport outside Osaka. All distribute leaflets on destinations throughout Japan and can provide train, bus, and ferry schedules and leaflets on major attractions and sights for example, Japanese gardens, hot springs, museums, and art galleries. They also carry information on hotels and *ryokan* and will book accommodations for you for free.

Local Information: You'll also find locally run tourist offices in nearly every city and town throughout Japan, most of them conveniently located at or near the main train station. Look for the logo of a red question mark with the word INFORMATION written below. Although the staff at a particular tourist office may not speak English (many do), they can point you in the direction of your hotel, perhaps provide you with an English-language map (usually free), and, in many cases, even make hotel bookings for you. Note, however, that they're not equipped to provide you with information on other regions of Japan (for that, go to a TIC). I've included information on local tourist offices throughout, including how to reach them after you disembark from the train and their open hours.

Entry Requirements & Customs

Passports

For most tourists, including those from the United States, Canada, Australia, New Zealand, and the United Kingdom, the only document necessary to enter Japan is a passport.

For information on obtaining passports, contact the following agencies:

For Residents of Australia: Contact the Australian Passport Information Service at tel. 131-232, or visit the government website at www.passports.gov.au.

For Residents of Canada: Contact the central Passport Office, Department of Foreign Affairs and International Trade, Ottawa, ON K1A 0G3
(tel. 800/567-6868; www.ppt.gc.ca).

For Residents of Ireland: Contact the Passport Office, Setanta Centre, Molesworth Street, Dublin 2 (tel. 01/671-1633; www.irlgov.ie/iveagh).

For Residents of New Zealand: Contact the Passports Office at tel. 0800/225-050 in New Zealand or 04/474-8100, or visit www.passports.govt.nz.

For Residents of the United Kingdom: Visit your nearest passport office, major post office, or travel agency or contact the United

Kingdom Passport Service at tel. 0870/521-0410 or visit www.ukpa.gov.uk.

For Residents of the United States: To find your regional passport office, check the U.S. State Department website (www.state.gov) or call the National Passport Information Center toll-free number (tel. 877/487-2778) for automated information.

Passport Savvy Safeguard your passport in an inconspicuous place and keep a photocopy of your passport's information page in your luggage. If you lose your passport, visit your nearest consulate as soon as possible for a replacement. Note: All foreigners must present their passports for bank transactions and for photocopying when checking into lodging facilities. In addition, foreigners are required to carry with them at all times either their passports or, for those who have been granted longer stays, their alien registration cards. Police generally do not stop foreigners, but if you're caught without an ID, you'll be taken to local police headquarters. It happened to me once and, believe me, I can think of better ways to spend an hour and a half than explaining in detail who I am, what I am doing in Japan, where I live, and what I plan to do for the rest of my life. I even had to write a statement explaining why I rushed out that day without my passport, apologizing and promising never to do such a thoughtless thing again. The policemen were polite and were simply doing their duty.

Entry Requirements

Americans, Australians, and New Zealanders traveling to Japan as tourists for a stay of 90 days or less need only a valid passport to gain entry into the country. Canadians don't need a visa for stays of up to 3 months, and United Kingdom and Irish citizens can stay up to 6 months without a visa.

Entry Procedures Since November 2007, all foreigners arriving in Japan are fingerprinted and photographed to prevent terrorists from entering Japan. Exceptions include children 15 and younger, diplomats, and some permanent residents of Japan.

Customs

If you're 20 or older, you can bring duty-free into Japan up to 400 non-Japanese cigarettes; three bottles (760cc each) of alcohol; and 2 ounces of perfume. You can also bring in goods for personal use that were purchased abroad whose total market value is less than ¥200,000.

What You Can Take Home from Japan For information on what you're allowed to bring home, contact one of the following agencies:

U.S. Citizens: U.S. Customs & Border Protection (CBP), 1300 Pennsylvania Ave., NW, Washington, DC 20229 (tel. 877/287-8667; www.cbp.gov).

Canadian Citizens: Canada Border Services Agency (tel. 800/461-9999 or 204/983-3500; www.cbsa-asfc.gc.ca).

U.K. Citizens: HM Customs & Excise (tel. 0845/010-9000, or 020/8929-0152 from outside the U.K.; www.hmce.gov.uk).

Australian Citizens: Australian Customs Service (tel. 1300/363-263;www.customs.gov.au).

New Zealand Citizens: New Zealand Customs, The Customhouse, 17-21 Whitmore St., Box 2218, Wellington (tel. 04/473-6099 or 0800/428-786; www.customs.govt.nz).

Medical Requirements

Unless you're arriving from an area known to be suffering from an epidemic (particularly cholera or yellow fever), inoculations or vaccinations are not required for entry into Japan. Note, however, that at the time of going to press, all arriving passengers are requested to fill out a questionnaire regarding symptoms of the H1N1 influenza such as fever or coughing. In addition, the temperature of all arriving passengers is taken upon entering the Customs area; if you have a fever, you may be quarantined as a protection against H1N1 or avian flu.

Hotels

Accommodations available in Japan range from Japanese-style inns to large Western-style hotels, in all price categories. Although you can travel throughout Japan without making reservations beforehand, it's essential to book in advance if you're traveling during peak travel seasons and is recommended at other times. If you arrive in a town without reservations, most local tourist offices generally located in or near the main train station will find accommodations for you at no extra charge. Note that in popular resort areas, most accommodations raise their rates during peak times. Some also charge more on weekends.

A note on reservations: When making reservations at Japanese-style accommodations and small business hotels, it's usually best if the call is conducted in Japanese or by fax or e-mail if available, as written English is always easier for most Japanese to understand. First-class hotels, however, always have English-speaking staff, as do many of the Japanese inns recommended in this guide.

A note about taxes and service charges: A 5% consumption tax is included in all hotel rates, including those given in this book.

Furthermore, upper-end hotels and some moderately priced hotels also add a 10% to 15% service charge to their published rates, while expensive ryokan will add a 10% to 20% service charge. No service charge is levied at business hotels, pensions, and minshuku (accommodations in a private home) for the simple reason that no services are provided. In resort areas with hot-spring spas, an *onsen* (spa) tax of ¥150 is added per night. Tokyo levies its own local hotel tax (¥100-¥200 per person per night). Unless otherwise stated, the prices given in this guide include all consumption taxes and service charge, but not onsen or local hotel tax.

Tips for Saving on Your Hotel Room

Although Japanese hotels traditionally remained pretty loyal to their published rack rates, which are always available at the front desk, the recession has opened possibilities for bargains.

Always ask politely whether there's a room less expensive than the first one offered: Because there are usually many categories, ask what the difference is, say, between a standard twin and a superior twin. If there are two of you, ask whether a double or a twin room is cheaper. Find out the hotel's policy on children do children stay free in the room or is there a special rate?

Contact the hotel directly: In addition to calling a hotel's toll-free number, call the hotel directly to see where you can get the best deal.

Check the Internet: Check to see whether discounts or special promotions are offered; some hotels offer discounts exclusively through the Internet.

Ask about promotions and special plans: Hotels frequently offer special "plans," including "Spring Plans," "Ladies' Plans," and even "Shopping Plans" that provide cheaper rates and services.

Remember the law of supply and demand: Resort hotels are more crowded and therefore more expensive on weekends and during peak travel periods such as Golden Week. Discounts, therefore, are often available for midweek and off-season stays. Business hotels, on the other hand, are sometimes cheaper on weekends.

Ask about hotel membership plans: Some chain business hotels offer hotel memberships with discounts on meals and free stays after a certain number of nights. Others, such as the New Otani, Okura, and the Imperial in Tokyo, allow free use of the hotel swimming pool simply if you become a member at no extra charge. Ask the concierge or front desk.

Finding a Hotel or Inn

If all my recommendations for a certain city are fully booked, or if you're traveling to destinations not covered in this guide, there are several ways to find alternative accommodations.

Surfing for Hotels: In addition to well-known booking sites like Travelocity, Expedia, Orbitz, and Hotels.com, you should also check Asia-specific sites like Asiatravel.com, Asia-hotels.com, and agoda.com. Of course, you'll also want to check all the websites mentioned earlier, such as www.j-hotel.or.jp for members of the Japan Hotel Association.

For budget accommodations, go to hostelworld.com, as well Rakuten Travel (tel. 050/2017-8977; www.travel.rakuten.co.jp/en), Japan's largest reservations company for budget and moderately priced accommodations. At the top of my list for budget accommodations are also members of Welcome Inns (www.itcj.jp), operated in cooperation with the Japan National Tourism Organization (JNTO) and International Tourism Center of Japan (ITCJ). Some 700 modestly priced accommodations, including business hotels and Japanese-style inns, are members of Welcome Inn, with rates no more than ¥8,000 for a single and ¥13,000 for a double. There's no fee for the service, but you must sign up for membership and guarantee your reservation with a credit card. Applications should be made about 2 weeks before desired check-in dates.

In any case, it's always a good idea to get a confirmation number and make a printout of any online booking transaction.

Finding a Room When You're in Japan In addition to booking Welcome Inns via the Internet, you can also book a room by visiting one of the three Tourist Information Centers in Japan at Narita Airport (in the arrivals lobbies of terminals 1 and 2); near Yurakucho Station in the heart of Tokyo; and at Osaka's Kansai International Airport, as well as Kyoto Tourist Information in Kyoto Station. Reservations are accepted at the Narita TIC daily from 8am to 7:30pm; at the Tokyo TIC daily from 9 to 11:30am and 1 to 4:30pm; in Kyoto daily from 10am to 12:30pm and 2 to 5:30pm (closed the 2nd and 4th Tues of every month); and at the Kansai TIC daily 8:30am to 8pm April to October and 9am to 8:30pm November to March.

High-end hotels and *ryokan* can be booked through travel agencies in Japan, including the ubiquitous Japan Travel Bureau.

Finally, if you arrive at your destination without accommodations, most major train stations contain a tourist information office or a hotel and ryokan reservation counter where you can book a room. Although policies may differ from office to office, you generally don't have to pay a fee for their services, but you usually do have to pay a percentage of your overnight charge as a deposit. The disadvantage is that you don't see the locale beforehand, and if there's space left at a ryokan even in peak tourist season, there may be a reason for it. Although these offices can be a real lifesaver in a pinch and in most cases may be able to recommend quite reasonable and pleasant places in which to stay, it pays to plan in advance.

Japanese-Style Accommodations

Japanese-Style Inns

Although an overnight stay in a *ryokan* (traditional Japanese inn) can be astoundingly expensive, it's worth the splurge at least once during your stay. Nothing quite conveys the simplicity and beauty indeed the very atmosphere of old Japan more than these inns with their gleaming polished wood, *tatami* floors, rice-paper sliding doors, and meticulously pruned gardens. Personalized service by kimono-clad hostesses and exquisitely prepared *kaiseki* meals are the trademarks of such inns, some of which are of ancient vintage. Indeed, staying in one is like taking a trip back in time.

If you want to experience a Japanese-style inn but can't afford the prices of a full-service ryokan, a number of alternatives are available. Although they don't offer the same personalized service, beautiful setting, or memorable cuisine, they do offer the chance to sleep on a futon in a simple tatami room and, in some cases, eat Japanese meals.

Ryokan Ryokan developed during the Edo Period, when *daimyo* (feudal lords) were required to travel to and from Edo (present-day Tokyo) every 2 years. They always traveled with a full entourage including members of their family, retainers, and servants. The best ryokan, of course, were reserved for the daimyo and members of the imperial family. Some of these exist today, passed down from generation to generation.

Traditionally, ryokan are small, only one or two stories high, contain about 10 to 30 rooms, and are made of wood with a tile roof. Most guests arrive at their ryokan around 3 or 4pm. The entrance is often through a gate and small garden; upon entering, you're met by a bowing woman in a kimono. Take off your shoes, slide on the proffered plastic slippers, and follow your hostess down the long wooden corridors until you reach the sliding door of your room. After taking off your slippers, step into your tatami room, almost void of furniture except for a low table in the middle of the room, floor cushions, an antique scroll hanging in a *tokonoma* (alcove), and a simple flower arrangement. Best of all is the view past rice-paper sliding screens of a Japanese landscaped garden with bonsai, stone lanterns, and a meandering pond filled with carp. Notice there's no bed in the room.

Almost immediately, your hostess serves you welcoming hot tea and a sweet at your low table so you can sit there for a while, recuperate from your travels, and appreciate the view, the peace, and the solitude. Next comes your hot bath, either in your own room (if you have one) or in the communal bath. Because many ryokan are clustered around onsen, many offer the additional luxury of bathing in thermal baths, including outdoor baths. After bathing and soaking away all travel fatigue, aches, and pains, change into your *yukata,* a cotton kimono provided by the ryokan. You can wear your yukata throughout the ryokan, even to its restaurant (in Western-style hotels, however, never wear a yukata outside your room unless you're going to its public bath).

When you return to your room, you'll find the maid ready to serve your *kaiseki* dinner, an elaborate spread that is the highlight of a ryokan stay. It generally consists of locally grown vegetables, sashimi (raw fish), grilled or baked fish, tempura, and various regional specialties, all spread out on many tiny plates; the menu is determined by the chef. Admire how each dish is in itself a delicate piece of artwork; it all looks too wonderful to eat, but finally hunger takes over.

If you want, you can order sake or beer to accompany your meal (but you'll pay extra for drinks).

After you've finished eating, your maid will return to clear away the dishes and to lay out your bed. The bed is really a futon, a kind of two-layered mattress with quilts, and is laid out on the tatami floor. The next morning, the maid will wake you, put away the futon, and serve a breakfast of fish, pickled vegetables, soup, dried seaweed, rice, and other dishes. Feeling rested, well fed, and pampered, you're then ready to pack your bags and pay your bill. Your hostess sees you off at the front gate, smiling and bowing as you set off for the rest of your travels.

Such is life at a good ryokan. Sadly, the number of upper-class ryokan diminishes each year. Unable to compete with more profitable high-rise hotels, many ryokan in Japan have closed down, especially in large cities; very few remain in such cities as Tokyo and Osaka. If you want to stay in a Japanese inn, it's best to do so in Kyoto, smaller towns like Takayama, or at a hot-spring spa.

In addition, although ideally a ryokan is an old wooden structure that once served traveling daimyo or was perhaps the home of a wealthy merchant, many today especially those in hot-spring resort areas are actually modern concrete affairs with as many as 100 or more rooms, with meals served in communal dining rooms. What they lack in intimacy and personal service, however, is made up for with cheaper prices and such amenities as modern bathing facilities and perhaps a bar and outdoor recreational facilities. Most guest rooms are fitted with a TV, a telephone, a safe for locking up valuables, and a cotton yukata, as well as such amenities as soap, shampoo, a razor, a toothbrush, and toothpaste.

Rates in a ryokan are always per person rather than per room and include breakfast, dinner, and often service and tax. Thus, while rates may seem high, they're actually competitively priced compared to what you'd pay for a hotel room and comparable meals in a restaurant. Although rates can vary from ¥9,000 to an astonishing ¥150,000 per person, the average cost is generally ¥12,000 to ¥20,000. Even within a single ryokan the rates can vary greatly, depending on the room you choose, the dinner courses you select, and the number of people in your room. If you're paying the highest rate, you can be certain you're getting the best room, the best view of the garden or perhaps even your own private garden, and a much more elaborate meal than lower-paying guests. All the rates for ryokan in this book are based on double occupancy; if there are more than two of you in one room, you can generally count on a slightly lower per-person rate; small children who sleep in the same bed as their parents often receive a discount as well. Although most Japanese would never dream of checking into an exclusive ryokan solo, lone travelers may be able to secure a room if it's not peak season.

Although I heartily recommend you try spending at least 1 night in a ryokan, there are a number of disadvantages to this style of accommodations. The most obvious problem is that you may find it uncomfortable sitting on the floor. And because the futon is put away during the day, there's no place to lie down for an afternoon nap or rest, except on the hard, tatami-covered floor. In addition, some of the older ryokan, though quaint, are bitterly cold in the winter and though increasingly rare may have only Japanese-style toilets. As for breakfast, you might find it difficult to swallow raw egg, rice, and seaweed in the morning. (I've even been served grilled grasshopper quite crunchy.) Sometimes you can get a Western-style breakfast if you order it the night before, but more often than not the fried or scrambled eggs will arrive cold, leading you to suspect they were cooked right after you ordered them.

A ryokan is also quite rigid in its schedule. You're expected to arrive sometime between 3 and 5pm, take your bath, and then eat at around 6 or 7pm. Breakfast is served early, usually by 8am, and checkout is by 10am. That means you can't sleep in, and because the maid is continually coming in and out, you have a lot less privacy than you would in a hotel.

Another drawback of the ryokan is that some will not take you. They simply do not want to deal with the problems inherent in accepting a foreign guest, including the language barrier and differing customs. I've seen a number of beautiful old ryokan I'd like to include in this book, but I've been turned away at the door. Sadly, I've also lost ryokan that once accepted foreigners but now refuse to do so because of unacceptable behavior (such as climbing in the window at midnight). In any case, those recommended in the pages that follow do welcome Westerners.

You should always make a reservation if you want to stay in a first-class ryokan (and even in most medium-priced ones), because the chef has to shop for and prepare your meals. Ryokan staff members often do not look kindly upon unannounced strangers turning up on their doorstep (though I did this on a weekday trip to Nikko without any problems at all). You can make a reservation for a ryokan through any travel agency in Japan or by contacting a ryokan directly. You may be required to pay a deposit. For more information on ryokan in Japan, including destinations not covered in this guide, pick up the *Japan Ryokan Guide* at one of the Tourist Information Centers in Japan, which lists some 1,300 members of the Japan Ryokan Association (tel. 03/3231-5310); or go online at www.ryokan.or.jp. Another useful resource is Japanese Guest Houses (www.japaneseguesthouses.com), with more than 600 member high-end and moderately priced Japanese inns.

Roller Bag Etiquette: I love my roller bag, but under no circumstances should you roll a bag on tatami or on old wooden floors of Japanese inns.

Japanese Inn Group: If you want the experience of staying in a Japanese-style room but cannot afford the extravagance of a ryokan, you might consider staying in one of the participating members of the Japanese Inn Group an organization of more than 80 Japanese-style inns and hotels throughout Japan offering inexpensive lodging and catering largely to foreigners. Although you may balk at the idea of staying at a place filled mainly with foreigners, keep in mind that some inexpensive Japanese-style inns are not accustomed to guests from abroad and may be quite reluctant to take you in. I have covered many Japanese Inn Group members in this book over the years and have found the owners for the most part to be an exceptional group of friendly people eager to offer foreigners the chance to experience life on tatami and futons. In many cases, these are good places in which to exchange information with other world travelers and are popular with both young people and families.

Although many of the group members call themselves ryokan, they are not ryokan in the true sense of the word, because they do not offer the trademark personalized service and only rarely the beautiful setting common to ryokan. However, they do offer simple tatami rooms that generally come with TVs and air conditioners; most have towels and cotton yukata. Some offer Western-style rooms as well, and/or rooms with private bathrooms. Facilities generally include a coin-operated washer and dryer, a public bath, and sometimes a computer for checking e-mail. The average cost of a 1-night stay is about ¥5,000 to ¥6,000 per person, without meals. Breakfast is usually available if you pay extra; dinner is also sometimes available.

You can view member inns at www.japaneseinngroup.com. Or, upon your arrival in Tokyo, head to the Tourist Information Center for the free pamphlet called *Japanese Inn Group*. Make reservations directly with the inn in which you wish to stay (most have faxes and e-mail). In some cases, you'll be asked to pay a deposit (most accept American Express, MasterCard, and Visa). Many member inns belong to the Welcome Inn Group as well, which means you can also make reservations through one of the methods described there.

Minshuku Technically, a *minshuku* is inexpensive Japanese-style lodging in a private home the Japanese version of a bed-and-breakfast. Usually located in tourist areas, rural settings, or small towns, minshuku can range from thatched farmhouses and rickety old wooden buildings to modern concrete structures. Because minshuku are family-run affairs, there's no personal service, which means you may be expected to lay out your own futon at night, stow it away in the morning, and tidy up your room. Most also do not supply a towel or *yukata,* nor do they have rooms with a private bathroom. There is, however, a public bathroom, and meals, included in the rates, are served in a communal dining room. Because minshuku cater primarily to domestic travelers, they're often excellent places to meet Japanese. Keep in mind, however, that many minshuku owners have day jobs, so it's important for guests to be punctual for meals and checkout.

Officially, what differentiates a ryokan from a minshuku is the level of service and corresponding price, but the differences are sometimes very slight. I've stayed in cheap ryokan providing almost no service and in minshuku too large and modern to be considered private homes. The average per-person cost for 1 night in a minshuku, including two meals, is generally ¥7,000 to ¥9,000 with two meals.

Reservations for minshuku should be made directly with the establishment. Or, contact the Minshuku Network Japan (tel. 0120/07-6556; www.minshuku.jp) for a reservation in one of its 3,000 members throughout Japan.

Kokumin Shukusha & Qkamura: A *kokumin shukusha* can be translated as a people's lodge public lodging found primarily in or around national parks and resort and vacation areas. Established by the government (though some are privately managed), there are more than 300 of these facilities throughout Japan. Catering largely to Japanese school groups and families, they offer basic, Japanese-style rooms at an average daily rate of about ¥8,000 to ¥9,000 per person, including two meals. Because they're usually full during the summer, peak seasons, holidays, and weekends, reservations are a must and can be made directly at the facility or through a travel agency; many are also in the *Directory of Welcome Inns*. There are also 36 National Park Resort Villages (nicknamed Qkamura; www.qkamura.or.jp) located exclusively in national parks and popular with families. The drawback for many of these lodges is that because they're often located in national parks and scenic spots, the best way to reach them is by car.

Shukubo: These are lodgings in a Buddhist temple, similar to inexpensive ryokan, except they're attached to temples and serve vegetarian food. There's usually an early morning service at 6am, which you're welcome in some *shukubo,* required to join. Probably the best place to experience life in a temple is at Mount Koya. Prices at shukubo generally range from about ¥7,000 to ¥15,000 per person, including two meals.

Western-Style Accommodations

Western-style lodgings range from luxurious first-class hotels to inexpensive ones catering primarily to Japanese businessmen.

When selecting and reserving your hotel room, contact the hotel directly to inquire about rates, even if a North American toll-free 800 number is provided; sometimes there are special deals, such as weekend or honeymoon packages, that central reservation desks are not aware of. Special rates are also often available only through the hotel's website. In any case, always ask what kinds of rooms are available. Almost all hotels in Japan offer a wide range of rooms at various prices, with room size the overwhelming factor in pricing. Other aspects that often have a bearing on rates include bed size, floor height (higher floors are more expensive), and in-room amenities. Rooms with views whether of the sea or a castle are also generally more expensive. In Japan, a twin room refers to a room with twin beds, and a double room refers to one with a double (or larger) bed; most hotels charge more for a twin room, but others charge more for doubles. Because Japanese couples generally prefer twin beds, doubles are often in short supply, especially in business hotels. A Hollywood twin means two twin beds pushed together side by side. *Note:* For the sake of convenience, the "double" rates for hotels listed in this guide refer to two people in one room and include both twin and double beds.

Some of the upper-priced hotels also offer executive floors, which are generally on the highest floors and may offer such perks as a private lounge with separate check-in, more in-room amenities, complimentary breakfast and evening cocktails, extended checkout time, and privileges that can include free use of the health club. At just a few thousand yen more than regular rates, these can be quite economical.

When making your reservation, therefore, inquire about the differences in room categories and rates and what they entail. Once you decide on the type of room you want, ask for the best in that category. For example, if you want a standard room, and deluxe rooms start on the 14th floor, ask for a standard on the 13th floor, which may give better views than standards on the 10th. In addition, be specific about the kind of room you want, whether it's a nonsmoking room, a room with a view of Mount Fuji, or a room with Internet connections for your laptop.

Be sure to give your approximate time of arrival, especially if it's after 6pm, when they might give your room away. Check-in ranges from about 1 or 2pm in first-class hotels to 3 or 4pm for business hotels. Checkout is generally about 10am for business hotels and 11am or noon for upper-range hotels. In any case, it's perfectly acceptable to leave luggage with the front desk or bell captain if you arrive early or want to sightsee after checking out.

Hotels: Both first-class and midpriced hotels in Japan are known for excellent service and cleanliness. The first-class hotels in the larger cities can compete with the best hotels in the world and offer a wide range of services, from health clubs and aesthetic spas with massage services to business centers and top-class restaurants and shopping arcades. Unfortunately, health clubs and swimming pools usually cost extra anywhere from ¥1,050 to an outrageous ¥5,000 per single use. In addition, outdoor pools are generally open only in July and August. Rooms come with such standard features as a minibar, bilingual cable TV with pay movies and English-language channels like CNN or BBC, high-speed Internet or wireless connections (usually at a charge at expensive hotels but often free in less expensive ones), clock, a radio, *yukata,* a hot-water pot and tea (and occasionally coffee, though you usually have to pay extra for it), a hair dryer, and a private bathroom with a tub/shower combination.

(Because Japanese are used to soaping down and rinsing off before bathing, it would be rare to find tubs without showers; similarly, showers without tubs are practically nonexistent in this nation of bathers.) Virtually all hotels nowadays also have "Washlet" toilets, which are combination toilets and spray bidets with a controllable range of speeds and temperatures. Because they're accustomed to foreigners, most hotels in this category employ an English-speaking staff and offer nonsmoking floors or rooms. Services provided include room service, same-day laundry and dry cleaning, and English-language newspapers such as the *Japan Times* delivered free to your room. Note that in medium-range hotels, same-day laundry service is not available Sundays and holidays and you must turn in your laundry by 10am to receive it by 5pm that day.

The most expensive hotels in Japan are in Tokyo and Osaka, where you'll pay at least ¥32,000 for a double or twin room in a first-class hotel and ¥16,000 to ¥32,000 for the same in a midpriced hotel.

Outside the major cities, rooms for two people range from about ¥20,000 to ¥30,000 for first-class hotels and ¥10,000 to ¥20,000 for midpriced hotels.

Although some internationally known high-end chains have a presence in Japan, including Four Seasons, Hyatt, and Ritz-Carlton, Japanese chains naturally dominate, including New Otani, Okura, Nikko, and JAL Hotels (associated with Japan Airlines), Prince, and the Japan Railways Group, which provides discounts to those with a Japan Rail Pass.

In addition to the recommendations in this guide, you can also check out the 400-some members of the Japan Hotel Association listed in the brochure *Hotels in Japan* available from the Tourist Information Centers in Japan or online at www.j-hotel.or.jp.

Business Hotels: Catering traditionally to traveling Japanese businessmen, a "business hotel" is a no-frills establishment with tiny, sparsely furnished rooms, most of them singles but usually with some twin and maybe double rooms also available. Primarily just places to crash for the night, these rooms usually have everything you need, but in miniature form minuscule bathroom, tiny bathtub/shower, small bed (or beds), empty fridge, and barely enough space to unpack your bags. If you're a large person, you may have trouble sleeping in a place like this. There are no bellhops, no room service, and sometimes not even a lobby or coffee shop, although usually there are vending machines selling beer, soda, cigarettes, and snacks. Most business hotels have nonsmoking rooms, but a few still do not. The advantages of staying in business hotels are price starting as low as ¥6,000 or ¥7,000 for a single and location usually near major train and subway stations. Check-in is usually not until 3 or 4pm, and checkout is usually at 10am; you can leave your bags at the front desk.

As for business-hotel chains, I'm partial to the Tokyo Inn chain, which boasts more than 160 locations around Japan and always employs female managers. They offer minuscule rooms outfitted with about everything you need, including free Internet access, and have raised the bar in business-hotel amenities by adding lobby computers with free Internet access, free domestic calls from lobby phones (but limited to 3 min.), usually free Japanese breakfast, and sometimes free nightly in-room movies (often in English). Other chains to look for are Tokyu Hotels, including its budget Tokyu Inns, all with specially designed Ladies Rooms with female-oriented toiletries and amenities, Washington Hotels, the Sunroute Hotel Chain, and newcomer Super Hotel with the lowest rates around.

Pensions: Pensions are like *minshuku,* except that accommodations are Western-style with beds instead of futons, and the two meals served are usually Western. Often managed by a young couple or a young staff, they cater to young Japanese and are most often located in ski resorts and in the countryside, sometimes making access a problem. Averaging 10 guest rooms, many seem especially geared to young Japanese women and are thus done up in rather feminine-looking decor with lots of pinks and flower prints. In recent years, *Wafu* Pensions (with Japanese-style rooms) have also made an appearance. The average cost is ¥8,000 per person per night, including two meals.

Youth Hostels: There are some 350 youth hostels in Japan, most of them privately run and operating in locations ranging from temples to concrete blocks. There's no age limit (though children 3 and younger may not be accepted), and although most of them require a youth hostel membership card, they let foreigners stay without one at no extra charge or for ¥600 extra per night (after 6 nights you automatically become a YH member). Youth hostels are reasonable, averaging about ¥3,000 per day without meals, and can be reserved in advance. However, there are usually quite a few restrictions, such as a 9 or 10pm curfew, a lights-out policy shortly thereafter, an early breakfast time, and closed times through the day, generally from about 10am to 3pm. In addition, rooms generally have many bunk beds or futons, affording little privacy. On the other hand, they're certainly the cheapest accommodations in Japan.

Because youth hostels are often inconveniently located, I have included only one, in Tokyo, but if you plan on staying almost exclusively in hostels, pick up a pamphlet called "Youth Hostel Map of Japan," available at the Tourist Information Centersin Japan, or check www.jyh.or.jp. For youth hostel membership in the U.S., contact Hostelling International USA (tel. 301/495-1240; www.hiusa.org).

Capsule Hotels: Capsule hotels, which became popular in the early 1980s, are used primarily by Japanese businessmen who have spent an evening out drinking and missed the last train home costing about ¥4,000 per person, a capsule hotel is sometimes cheaper than a taxi to the suburbs. Units are small no larger than a coffin and consisting of a bed, a private TV, an alarm clock, and a radio and are usually stacked two deep in rows down a corridor; the only thing separating you from your probably inebriated neighbor is a curtain. A cotton kimono and a locker are provided, and bathrooms and toilets are communal. Most capsule hotels do not accept women, but those that do have separate facilities.

Love Hotels: Finally, a word about Japan's so-called "love hotels." Usually found close to entertainment districts and along major highways, such hotels do not provide sexual services themselves; rather, they offer rooms for rent by the hour to couples. You'll know that you've wandered into a love-hotel district when you notice hourly rates posted near the front door, though gaudy structures shaped like ocean liners or castles are also a dead giveaway. Because many of them have reasonable overnight rates as well, I have friends who, finding themselves out too late and too far from home, have checked into love hotels, solo.

When to Go

Because Japan stretches in an arc from northeast to southwest at about the same latitudes as Maine and Florida, you can travel in the country virtually any time of year. Winters in southern Kyushu and Okinawa are mild, while summers in northern Hokkaido are cool. There are, however, peak seasons to avoid, including April 29 to May 5, mid-July through August, and New Year's.

Climate: Most of Japan's islands lie in a temperate seasonal wind zone similar to that of the East Coast of the United States, which means there are four distinct seasons. Japanese are very proud of their seasons and place much more emphasis on them than people do in the West. Kimono, dishes and bowls used for *kaiseki,* and even *noh* plays change with the season. Certain foods are eaten during certain times of the year, such as eel in summer and *fugu* (blowfish) in winter. Almost all haiku have seasonal references. The cherry blossom signals the beginning of spring, and most festivals are tied to seasonal rites. Even urban dwellers note the seasons; almost as though on cue, businessmen will change virtually overnight from their winter to summer attire.

Summer: which begins in June, is heralded by the rainy season, which lasts from about mid-June to mid-July (there's no rainy season in Hokkaido). Although it doesn't rain every day, it does rain a lot, sometimes quite heavily, making umbrellas imperative. After the rain stops, it turns unbearably hot and uncomfortably humid throughout the country, with the exception of Hokkaido, mountaintop resorts such as Hakone, and the Japan Alps. You'll be more comfortable in light cottons, though you should bring a light jacket for unexpected cool evenings or air-conditioned rooms. You should also pack sunscreen and a hat (Japanese women are also fond of parasols).

The period from the end of August to September is typhoon season, although the majority of storms stay out at sea and generally vent their fury on land only in thunderstorms.

Autumn: lasting through November, is one of the best times to visit Japan. The days are pleasant and slightly cool, and the changing red and scarlet of leaves contrast brilliantly with the deep blue skies. There are many chrysanthemum shows in Japan at this time, popular maple-viewing spots, and many autumn festivals. Bring a warm jacket.

Winter: lasting from December to March, is marked by snow in much of Japan, especially in the mountain ranges where the skiing is superb. Many tourists also flock to hot-spring resorts during this time. The climate is generally dry, and on the Pacific coast the skies are often blue. Tokyo doesn't get much snow, though it can be crisp, cold, and wet. Northern Japan's weather, in Tohoku and Hokkaido, can be quite severe, while southern Japan, especially Kyushu and Okinawa, enjoys generally mild, warm weather. Wherever you are, you'd be wise to bring warm clothing throughout the winter months.

Spring: arrives with a magnificent fanfare of plum and cherry blossoms in March and April, an exquisite time when all of Japan is ablaze in whites and pinks. The cherry-blossom season starts in southern Kyushu in mid-March and reaches Hokkaido in early May. The blossoms themselves last only a few days, symbolizing to Japanese the fragile nature of beauty and of life itself. Other flowers also bloom through May or June, including azaleas and irises. During spring, numerous festivals throughout Japan celebrate the rebirth of nature.

Busy Seasons: Japanese have a passion for travel, and they generally travel at the same time, resulting in jampacked trains and hotels. The worst times to travel are around New Year's, from the end of December to January 4; Golden Week, from April 29 to May 5; and during the Obon Festival, about a week in mid-August. Avoid traveling on these dates at all costs, since all long-distance trains, domestic airlines, and most accommodations are booked solid and prices are higher. The weekends before and after these holidays are also likely to be crowded or booked. Exceptions are major cities like Tokyo or Osaka since the major exodus is back to hometowns or the countryside, metropolises can be downright blissful during major holidays such as Golden Week, especially since most restaurants and municipal and national museums do not close.

Another busy time is during the school summer vacation, from around July 19 or 20 through August. It's best to reserve train seats and book accommodations during this time in advance. In addition, you can expect destinations to be packed during major festivals, so if one of these is high on your list, be sure to make plans well in advance.

Holidays: National holidays are January 1 (New Year's Day), second Monday in January (Coming-of-Age Day), February 11 (National Foundation Day), March 20 (Vernal Equinox Day), April 29 (Showa Day, after the late Emperor Showa), May 3 (Constitution Memorial Day), May 4 (Greenery Day), May 5 (Children's Day), third Monday in July (Maritime Day), third Monday in September (Respect-for-the-Aged Day), September 23 (Autumn Equinox Day), second Monday in October (Health Sports Day), November 3 (Culture Day), November 23 (Labor Thanksgiving Day), and December 23 (Emperor's Birthday).

When a national holiday falls on a Sunday, the following Monday becomes a holiday. Although government offices and some businesses are closed on public holidays, restaurants and most stores remain open. The exception is during the New Year's celebration, January 1 through January 3 or 4, when virtually all restaurants, public and private offices, stores, and even ATMs close; during that time, you'll have to dine in hotels.

All museums close for New Year's for 1 to 4 days, but most major museums remain open for the other holidays. If a public holiday falls on a Monday (when most museums are closed), many museums will remain open but will close instead the following day, Tuesday. Note, however, that privately owned museums, such as art museums or special-interest museums, generally close on public holidays. To avoid disappointment, be sure to phone ahead if you plan to visit a museum on a holiday or the day following it.

Festivals: With Shintoism and Buddhism the major religions in Japan, it seems as though there's a *matsuri* (festival) going on somewhere in the country almost every day, especially in summer. Every major shrine and temple has at least one annual festival. Such festivals are always free, though admission may be charged for special exhibitions such as flower shows. There are also a number of national holidays observed throughout the country with events and festivals, as well as annual seasonal events like cormorant fishing and cherry-blossom viewing.

The larger, better-known festivals are exciting to attend but do take some advance planning since hotel rooms may be booked 6 months in advance. If you haven't made prior arrangements, you may want to let the following schedule be your guide in avoiding certain cities on certain days.

A note on festival dates: If you plan your trip around a certain festival, be sure to double-check the exact dates with the Japan National Tourist Organization since these dates can change. In Japan, stop by a TIC office in Tokyo or at Narita or Kansai airports for a monthly leaflet called "Calendar Events," which lists major festivals in Tokyo and the rest of Japan. You can also try calling the local tourist office of the city hosting the festival (though staff may not speak much English) or checking JNTO and local websites for information.

Getting There

By Plane

Japan has three international airports. Outside Tokyo is Narita International Airport (NRT), where you'll want to land if your main business is in the capital, the surrounding region, or at points north or east such as Hokkaido. Another international airport, Kansai International Airport (KIX) outside Osaka, is convenient if your destination is Osaka, Kobe, Nara, Kyoto, or western or southern Japan; it is also convenient for domestic air travel within Japan, since most domestic flights out of Tokyo depart from Haneda Airport, necessitating an airport transfer if you arrive at Narita International Airport. In between Narita and Kansai airports, outside Nagoya, is the Central Japan International Airport (NGO), nicknamed Centrair, which offers the advantage of slick airport facilities (including hot-spring baths!) and easy access to Nagoya, the Shinkansen bullet train, Japan Alps, and beyond.

Because the flight to Tokyo is such a long one (about 12 hr. from Los Angeles or London and 13 1/2 hr. from Chicago or New York), you may wish to splurge for a roomier seat and upgraded service, including special counters for check-in, private lounges at the airport, and better meals, though these come with a price. You should also consider a mileage program, because you'll earn lots of miles going to Japan.

Japan's major carriers are Japan Airlines (JAL) and All Nippon Airways (ANA).JAL, Japan's flagship and largest domestic carrier, offers more international flights to Japan than any other airline, flying nonstop to Tokyo from Honolulu, Kona, Los Angeles, San Francisco, Chicago, New York, and Vancouver. JAL also serves other countries worldwide, including flights from London, Sydney, and Auckland to Tokyo. ANA offers daily nonstop service from New York, Washington, D.C., Chicago, Seattle, Los Angeles, San Francisco, Honolulu, Toronto, Vancouver, and London.

One advantage to flying with JAL or ANA to Japan is that you can purchase your Japan Rail Pass through them. In addition, flying to Japan with JAL (or another Oneworld fare partner such as American Airlines) or ANA (or a Star Alliance member such as United Airlines) means you are then eligible for deep discounts on domestic flights within Japan.

Getting Around

Japan has an extensive transport system, the most convenient segment of which is the nation's excellent rail service. You can also travel by plane (good for long-distance hauls but expensive unless you plan ahead), bus (the cheapest mode of travel), ferry, and car.

By Train

The most efficient way to travel around most of Japan is by train. Whether you're being whisked through the countryside aboard the famous Shinkansen bullet train or are winding your way up a wooded mountainside in an electric streetcar, trains in Japan are punctual, comfortable, safe, and clean. All trains except local commuters have washrooms, toilets, and drinking water. Bullet trains even have telephones and carts selling food and drinks. And because train stations are usually located in the heart of the city next to the city bus terminal or a subway station, arriving in a city by train is usually the most convenient method. Furthermore, most train stations in Japan's major cities and resort areas have tourist offices. The staff may not speak English, but they usually have maps or brochures in English and can point you in the direction of your hotel. Train stations also may have a counter where hotel reservations can be made free of charge. Most of Japan's passenger trains are run by six companies (such as JR East and JR Kyushu) that make up the Japan Railways (JR) Group. There are also private regional companies, like Kintetsu (Kinki Nippon

Railway) operating around Osaka, Kyoto, Nagoya, and Ise and Odakyu Electric Railway operating from Tokyo to Hakone.

Shinkansen (Bullet Train): The Shinkansen is probably Japan's best-known train. With a front car that resembles a space rocket, the Shinkansen hurtles along at a maximum speed of 300kmph (187 mph) through the countryside on its own special tracks.

There are five basic Shinkansen routes in Japan, plus some offshoots. The most widely used line for tourists is the Tokaido Shinkansen, which runs from Tokyo and Shinagawa stations west to such cities as Nagoya, Kyoto, and Osaka. The Sanyo Shinkansen extends westward from Osaka through Kobe, Himeji, Okayama, and Hiroshima before reaching its final destination in Hakata/Fukuoka on the island of Kyushu.

Only *Nozomi Super Express* Shinkansen, the fastest and most frequent trains, cover the entire 1,179km (730 miles) between Tokyo and Hakata. The *Hikari* makes more stops than the Nozomi; the *Kodama* stops at every station. Frustratingly, the *Nozomi* is not covered by the Japan Rail Pass, so rail-pass travelers wishing to go the entire distance must take the Hikari or Kodama and transfer in Osaka or Okayama. Trains run so frequently as often as four times an hour during peak times not including the *Nozomi* that it's almost like catching the local subway.

The Tohoku Shinkansen Line runs north from Tokyo and Ueno stations to Sendai, Morioka, Kakunodate, and Hachinohe (some trains require reservations), with branches extending to Shinjo and Akita. By 2011, the Akita branch will extend farther north all the way to Aomori, with future plans calling for a new Hokkaido Shinkansen to extend all the way to Sapporo by 2013. The Joetsu Shinkansen connects Tokyo and Ueno stations with Niigata on the Japan Sea coast, while the Nagano Shinkansen,completed in time for the 1998 Winter Olympics, connects Tokyo and Ueno stations with Nagano in the Japan Alps. The newest line is the Kyushu Shinkansen, which currently runs between Shin-Yatsuhiro and Kagoshima but will extend all the way from Kagoshima to Hakata by 2011.

Shinkansen running along these lines usually offer two or more kinds of service trains that stop only at major cities (like the Nozomi on the Tokaido-Sanyo Line) and trains that make more stops and are therefore slightly slower. Note: If your destination is a smaller city on the Shinkansen line, make sure the train you take stops there. As a plus, each stop is announced in English through a loudspeaker and a digital signboard in each car.

Regular Service: In addition to bullet trains, there are also two types of long-distance trains that operate on regular tracks. The limited-express trains, or LEX *(Tokkyu),* branch off the Shinkansen system and are the fastest after the bullet trains, often traveling scenic routes, while the express trains *(Kyuko)* are slightly slower and make more stops. Slower still are rapid express trains *(Shin-Kaisoku)* and the even slower rapid trains *(Kaisoku).* To serve the everyday needs of Japan's commuting population, local trains *(Futsu)* stop at all stations.

For long distances, say, between Tokyo and Sapporo, JR operates overnight sleeper **trains** *(Shindai-sha),* which offer compartments and berths.

Information: For the most comprehensive site covering rail travel in Japan, go to www.japanrailpass.net, which also provides links to the websites of all six JR Group companies, gives fares and timetables for long-distance JR trains (including the Shinkansen), displays maps of Tokyo and Shinjuku stations, and contains information on rail passes. I also like www.hyperdia.com and www.jorudan.co.jp, both of which give routes (including transfers), fares, and timetables for trains and planes in Japan.

In Japan, stop by the Tourist Information Center in downtown Tokyo or at the international airports in Narita or Osaka for the invaluable

Railway Timetable, published in English and providing train schedules for the Shinkansen and limited express JR lines throughout Japan. To be on the safe side, I also stop by the train information desk or the tourist information desk as soon as I arrive in a city to check on train schedules onward to my next destination. Another good resource is the JR East InfoLine (tel. 050/2016-1603; www.jreast.co.jp/e), available daily 10am to 6pm to answer questions about train schedules, fares, how to buy tickets, and more.

Train Distances & Traveling Time Japan is much longer than most people imagine. Its four main islands, measured from the northeast to the southwest, cover roughly the distance from Boston to Atlanta. Thank goodness for the Shinkansen bullet train! In addition, transportation can be slow in mountainous regions, especially if you're on a local train.

Train Fares & Reservations Ticket prices are based on the type of train (Shinkansen bullet trains are the most expensive), the distance traveled, whether your seat is reserved, and the season, with slightly higher prices (usually a ¥200 surcharge) during peak seasons (Golden Week, July 21-Aug 31, Dec 25-Jan 10, and Mar 21-Apr 5). Children (ages 6-11) pay half fare, while up to two children 5 and younger travel free if they do not require a separate seat. I've included train prices from Tokyo for many destinations covered. Unless stated otherwise, prices in this guide are for adults for nonreserved seats on the fastest train available (except the *Nozomi*) during regular season. You can buy JR tickets and obtain information about JR trains traveling throughout Japan at any Japan Railways station (in Tokyo this includes major stations along the Yamanote Line, which loops around Tokyo). If you wish to purchase a ticket using a credit card, go to a Ticket Reservation Office *(Midori-no-madoguchi)* at any major JR station.

No matter which train you ride, be sure to hang onto your ticket you'll be required to give it up at the end of your trip as you exit through the gate.

Seat Reservations: You can reserve seats for the Shinkansen, as well as for limited-express and express trains (but not for slower rapid or local trains, which are on a first-come, first-served basis) at any major Japan Railways station in Japan. Reserved seats cost slightly more than unreserved seats (¥300-¥510 for the Shinkansen and express trains). The larger stations have a special reservation counter called Midori-no-madoguchi (Ticket Reservation Office) or View Plaza (Travel Service Center), easily recognizable by their green signs with RESERVATION TICKETS written on them. If you're at a JR station with no special reservation office, you can reserve your seats at one of the regular ticket windows. You can also purchase and reserve seats at several travel agents, including the giant Japan Travel Bureau (JTB), which has offices all over Japan. Finally, JR East (serving the area around Tokyo and north through Tohoku) offers Internet reservation for its trains at http://jreast-shinkansen-reservation.eki-net.com; unfortunately, the reservation system does not apply to lines run by other JR companies, including the popular Tokaido/Sanyo Shinkansen to Kyoto and beyond.

It's a good idea to reserve your seats for your entire trip through Japan as soon as you know your itinerary if you'll be traveling during peak times; however, you can only reserve 1 month in advance. If it's not peak season, you'll probably be okay using a more flexible approach to traveling all trains also have nonreserved cars that fill up on a first-come, first-seated basis. You can also reserve seats on the day of travel up to departure time. I hardly ever reserve a seat when it's not peak season, preferring instead the flexibility of being able to hop on the next available train (or, sometimes I reserve a seat just before boarding). If you want to sit in the nonsmoking car of the Shinkansen bullet train, ask for the *kinensha,* though nowadays most trains are completely smoke free.

Tips for Saving Money: If your ticket is for travel covering more than 100km (62 miles), you can make as many stopovers en route as you wish as long as you complete your trip within the period of the ticket's validity. Tickets for 100 to 200km (62-124 miles) are valid for 2 days, with 1 day added for each additional 200km. Note, too, that stopovers are granted only for trips that are not between major urban areas, such as Tokyo, Yokohama, Osaka, Nagoya, Kyoto, Kobe, Hiroshima, Kitakyushyu, Fukuoka, Sendai, or Sapporo. In addition, stopovers are not permitted when traveling by express and limited express. Ask about stopovers when purchasing your ticket.

You can also save money by purchasing a round-trip ticket for long distances. A round-trip ticket by train on distances exceeding 600km (373 miles) one-way costs 20% less than two one-way tickets.

If you don't qualify for a Japan Rail Pass, the Seishun 18 (Seishun ju-hachi kippu)is a 5-day rail pass for ¥11,500 for travel anywhere in Japan as long as you use JR local and rapid trains (that is, no Shinkansen, limited express, or express trains), making it a good bet for day excursions in the countryside, albeit very slow ones (the trip from Tokyo to Kyoto would take 9 hr. and requires three or more changes of trains, compared to 2 hr. 20 min. on the Shinkansen). The biggest drawback, however, is that it's available only during Japan's three major school holidays: spring break (Mar 1-Apr 10); summer break (July 20-Sept 10); and winter break (Dec 10-Jan 10). You can use it on 5 consecutive days or on any 5 days within the school break period; people traveling together can share the five rides (for example, two people can travel for 2 days and one person can travel for 1 day).

There are also regional tickets good for sightseeing. The Hakone Free Pass, for example, offered by Odakyu railways (www.odakyu.jp/english), includes round-trip transportation from Tokyo and unlimited travel in Hakone for a specific number of days. The Hokkaido Furii Pasu (www.jrhokkaido.co.jp) valid for 7 days of JR train and bus travel in Hokkaido, costs ¥25,500, though some restrictions apply. There are also special passes for seniors (Full Moon Pass, valid for married couples with a combined total age of 88) and for two or three women age 30 and over traveling as a group (Nice Midi Pass). If you qualify, the Japan Rail Pass, however, is a better deal than these alternatives.

Japan Rail Pass: The Japan Rail Pass is without a doubt the most convenient and most economical way to travel around Japan. With the rail pass, you don't have to worry about buying individual tickets, and you can reserve your seats on all JR trains for free. The rail pass entitles you to unlimited travel on all JR train lines including the Shinkansen (except, regrettably, the *Nozomi Super Express*), as well as on most JR buses and the JR ferry to Miyajima.

There are several types of rail passes available; make your decision based on your length of stay in Japan and the cities you intend to visit. You might even find it best to combine several passes to cover your travels in Japan, such as a 1-week standard pass for longer journeys, say, to Kyushu, plus a regional pass just for Kyushu. Online pass information is available at www.japanrailpass.net.

The Standard Pass: If you wish to travel throughout Japan, your best bet is to purchase the standard Japan Rail Pass. It's available for ordinary coach class and for the first-class Green Car and is available for travel lasting 1, 2, or 3 weeks. Rates for the ordinary pass (as of Jan 2010) are ¥28,300 for 7 days, ¥45,100 for 14 days, and ¥57,700 for 21 days. Rates for the Green Car are ¥37,800, ¥61,200, and ¥79,600 respectively. Children (ages 6-11) pay half fare. Personally, I have never traveled in the first-class Green Car in Japan and don't consider it necessary. However, during peak travel times (New Year's, Golden Week, and Obon in mid-Aug), you may find it easier to reserve a seat in the first-class Green Car, which you can get by paying a surcharge in addition to showing your ordinary pass.

Before You Leave Home The standard Japan Rail Pass is available only to foreigners visiting Japan as tourists and *can be purchased only outside Japan.* It's available from most travel agents, including Kintetsu

International (tel. 800/422-3481; www.kintetsu.com) and JTB USA (tel. 800/235-3523; www.jtbusa.com). If you're flying Japan Airlines (JAL; tel. 800/525-3663; www.ar.jal.com/en) or All Nippon Airways (ANA; tel. 800/235-9262; www.ana.co.jp), you can also purchase a rail pass from them. A full list of authorized travel agents is available at www.japanrailpass.net.

Upon purchasing your pass, you'll be issued a voucher (called an Exchange Order), which you'll then exchange for the real pass after your arrival in Japan. Note that once you purchase your Exchange Order, you have 3 months until you must exchange it in Japan for the pass itself. When obtaining your actual pass, you must then specify the date you wish to start using the pass within a 1-month period.

Once You've Arrived: In Japan, you can exchange your voucher for a Japan Rail Pass at more than 40 JR stations that have Japan Rail Pass exchange offices, at which time you must present your passport and specify the date you wish to begin using the pass; most offices are open daily from 10am to 6 or 7pm, some even longer.

At both Narita Airport (daily 6:30am-9:45pm) and Kansai International Airport (daily 6:30am-9:45pm), you can pick up Japan Rail Passes at either the Travel Service Center or the Ticket Office. Other Travel Service Centers or Ticket Offices, all located in JR train stations, include those at Tokyo (daily 5:30am-10:45pm), Ueno, Shinjuku, Ikebukuro, Shibuya, and Shinagawa stations in Tokyo; Kyoto Station; Shin-Osaka and Osaka stations; and Sapporo, Hakodate, Nagoya, Kanazawa, Okayama, Matsue, Hiroshima, Takamatsu, Matsuyama, Hakata, Nagasaki, Kumamoto, and Kagoshima Chuo stations. Stations and their open hours are listed in a pamphlet you'll receive with your voucher.

Regional Passes for Foreign Visitors: In addition to the standard Japan Rail Pass above, there are regional JR rail passes available for ordinary coach class that are convenient for travel in eastern or western Honshu, Kyushu, or Hokkaido. They can be purchased before arriving in Japan from the same vendors that sell the standard pass. All but the Kintetsu Rail Pass can also be purchased inside Japan, usually only within the area covered by the pass but also at Narita airport for some passes. These regional passes are available only to foreign visitors and require that you present your passport to verify your status as a "temporary visitor"; you may also be asked to show your plane ticket. Only one pass per region per visit to Japan is allowed.

If you're arriving by plane at the Kansai Airport outside Osaka and intend to remain in western Honshu, you may opt for one of two different JR-West Passes(www.westjr.co.jp/english), available at Kansai Airport, Osaka JR station, and other locations. The Kansai Area

Pass, which can be used for travel between Osaka, Kyoto, Kobe, Nara, Himeji, and other destinations in the Kansai area, is available as a 1-day pass for ¥2,000, 2-day pass for ¥4,000, 3-day pass for ¥5,000, or 4-day pass for ¥6,000. Travel is restricted to JR rapid and local trains, as well as unreserved seating in limited express trains that operate only between Kansai Airport, Shin-Osaka, and Kyoto (that is, Shinkansen are not included in the pass). Children pay half-price for all passes. The other JR-West Pass available is the Sanyo Area Pass, which covers a larger area, allows travel via Shinkansen (including the superfast *Nozomi*) and JR local trains from Osaka as far as Hakata (in the city of Fukuoka on Kyushu), and includes Hiroshima, Okayama, Kurashiki, Himeji, and Kobe. It's available for 4 days for ¥20,000 and for 8 days for ¥30,000.

There are also a couple other non-JR passes available for Kansai. The Kansai Thru Pass (www.surutto.com) is valid on city subways, private railways (*not* JR trains), and buses throughout the Kansai area. Available only to tourists, it costs ¥3,800 for a 2-day pass and ¥5,000 for 3 days and is sold at Kansai International Airport and Tourist Information Centers in Osaka and Nara. Or, if you plan to spend a few days traveling farther afield between Nagoya, Osaka, Kyoto, and Ise-Shima, you can save money by purchasing a Kintetsu Rail Pass (www.kintetsu.co.jp), which covers travel throughout the region on

Kintetsu's private lines. Available only for foreigners, it must be purchased before arriving in Japan at Kintetsu offices or authorized travel agencies. It costs ¥3,500 and includes 5 days of unlimited travel (but only 3 trips on limited express trains). For ¥5,700, you can purchase the Kintetsu Rail Pass Wide, which adds a trip from Centrair or Kansai Airport, Mie Kotsu buses, and discount coupons for sightseeing spots.

Though not as popular as western Honshu, eastern Honshu also offers its own JR-East Pass (www.jreast.co.jp), which includes travel from Tokyo to Nagano in the Japan Alps and throughout the Tohoku District, including Sendai, Kakunodate, and Aomori via Shinkansen and local JR lines. Passes for travel in ordinary coach cars are available for 5 days for ¥20,000 and 10 days for ¥32,000; a 4-day flexible pass (valid for any 4 consecutive or nonconsecutive days within a month) costs ¥20,000. Green Car passes are also available. Passes are available at Narita airport and JR stations in Tokyo, including Tokyo, Shinagawa, and Shinjuku, as well as online at http://jreast-shinkansen-reservation.eki-net.com.

If your travels are limited to the island of Kyushu, consider the JR-Kyushu Rail Pass(www.jrkyushu.co.jp), valid for 3 days for ¥13,000 (¥7,000 for northern Kyushu only) and for 5 days for ¥16,000 and available for purchase at Narita Airport and at Hakata, Nagasaki, Kumamoto, Kagoshima Chuo, and Beppu JR stations. Likewise, there's a Hokkaido Rail Pass (www.jrhokkaido.co.jp) valid for 3 days of travel for ¥15,000 or 5 days (or 4 flexible days within a 10-day period) for ¥19,500, sold at Narita Airport and Hakodate and Sapporo JR stations.

By Plane

Because it takes the better part of a day and night to travel by train from Tokyo down to southern Kyushu or up to northern Hokkaido, you may find it faster not to mention cheaper if you buy your ticket in advance to fly at least one stretch of your journey in Japan. You could, for example, fly internationally into Osaka and then onward to Fukuoka on Kyushu, from where you can take a leisurely 2 weeks to travel by train through Kyushu and Honshu before returning to Osaka. I don't, however, advise flying short distances say, from Tokyo to Osaka simply because the time spent getting to and from airports is longer than the time spent traveling by Shinkansen.

Almost all domestic flights from Tokyo leave from the much more conveniently located Haneda Airport. If you're already in Tokyo, you can easily reach Haneda Airport via Airport Limousine Bus, monorail from Hamamatsucho Station on the Yamanote Line, or the Keikyu Line from Shinagawa. If you're arriving on an international flight at Narita

Airport, therefore, make sure you know whether a connection to a domestic flight is at Narita or requires a transfer to Haneda Airport via the Airport Limousine Bus.

Two major domestic airlines are Japan Airlines (JAL; tel. 0570/025-071 in Japan; www.jal.co.jp) and All Nippon Airways (ANA; tel. 0570/029-709 in Japan; www.ana.co.jp). Regular fares with these two companies are generally the same no matter which airline you fly domestically and are more expensive for peak season including New Year's, Golden Week, and summer vacation. However, bargains do exist. Some flights early in the day or late at night may be cheaper than flights during peak time; there are also discounts for seniors 65 and over. Your best bet on snagging a discount, however, is to purchase your ticket in advance. ANA's *Tabiwari* and JAL's *Sakitoku* are discount fares on reservations made 28 days in advance, while the Super Tabiwari and Super Saitoku give deep discounts on tickets purchased 45 days in advance. Regular one-way fares from Tokyo to Naha, Okinawa, for example, are ¥40,900 but go as low as ¥12,800 for a Super Tabiwari or Super Saitoku on selected flights. There are also slight discounts on tickets booked 3 to 7 days before departure and on round-trip fares.

Otherwise, there are small regional airlines that generally offer fares that are cheaper than the standard full fare charged by JAL or ANA.

These include Skymark (tel. 03/3433-7670 in Tokyo, or 092/736-3131 in Fukuoka; www.skymark.co.jp), operating out of Fukuoka; Skynet Asia Airways (tel. 0120/737-283 toll-free; www.skynetasia.co.jp), connecting Nagasaki, Kumamoto, and Kagoshima with Tokyo and Okinawa; and Air Do (tel. 0120/0570-333 toll-free), out of Sapporo.

For information on fares from Tokyo to major cities throughout Japan, see individual city listings in this guide. Tickets can be purchased directly through the airline or at a travel agent such as Japan Travel Bureau (JTB), which has offices virtually everywhere in Japan.

Special Domestic Fares for Foreigners Purchasing domestic tickets in advance in connection with your international flight is by far the most economical way to go. JAL's "Oneworld Yokoso/Visit Japan Fare" ticket, purchased in conjunction with a flight to Japan with JAL or one of its Oneworld fare partners (such as American Airlines) and sold only outside Japan, provides discount fares of ¥10,000 per flight for domestic travel to 42 cities in Japan served by JAL and its two subsidiaries, JAL Express and Japan Transocean Air (JTA).

Visitors flying other airlines into Japan can take advantage of JAL's "Welcome to Japan Fare," which provides discounts on JAL's domestic flights regardless of which international airline is used to reach Japan.

Also sold only outside Japan, this costs ¥13,650 per flight, with a minimum of two flights required.

ANA offers a similar program, with its Star Alliance Japan Airpass ticket costing ¥11,000 per flight if you fly ANA or one of its Star Alliance partners such as United Airlines; if you fly another airline, its Visit Japan Fare is ¥13,000 per ticket. Note that there are blackout dates for all these fares, mostly in mid-March, during summer vacation (mid-July through Aug), and New Year's, and that fares exclude airport taxes and insurance. You should first purchase your international ticket and then contact JAL or ANA to purchase and book your Japan domestic tickets.

If you plant to visit at least two Okinawan islands in addition to Okinawa Island, you can save money by purchasing an Okinawa Island Pass, valid on five specific routes within the Okinawan island chain, including flights from Naha to Kume or Ishigaki, on Japan Transocean Air (a subsidiary of JAL). A minimum of two flights, at ¥9,000 each, is required, and tickets must be purchased from JAL before arriving in Japan. For more information, contact your nearest JAL office.

By Bus

Buses often go where trains don't and thus may be the only way for you to get to the more remote areas of Japan, such as Shirakawa-go in the Japan Alps. In Hokkaido, Tohoku, Kyushu, and other places, buses are used extensively.

Some intercity buses require you to make reservations or purchase your ticket in advance at the ticket counter at the bus terminal. For others (especially local buses), when you board a bus you'll generally find a ticket machine by the entry door. Take a ticket, which is number-coded with a digital board displayed at the front of the bus. The board shows the various fares, which increase with the distance traveled. You pay when you get off.

In addition to serving the remote areas of the country, long-distance buses (called *chokyori basu*) also operate between major cities in Japan and offer the cheapest mode of transportation. Although Japan Railways operates almost a dozen bus routes eligible for JR Rail Pass coverage, the majority of buses are run by private companies (most of which do not have English-language websites). Some long-distance buses travel during the night and offer reclining seats and toilets, thus saving passengers the price of a night's lodging. Long-distance buses departing from Tokyo Station, for example, cost ¥4,200 to ¥8,600 for Kyoto or Osaka, depending on the company and time of day, and

¥12,060 for Hiroshima. Long-distance bus tickets can be purchased at View Plazas at major JR stations (for JR buses), at travel agencies such as JTB, or at bus terminals.

For more information on local and long-distance bus service, refer to individual cities covered in this guide, contact the Tourist Information Center in Tokyo or the local tourist office, or check the websites www.bus.or.jp, www.jrbuskanto.co.jp, and http://willerexpress.com.

By Car

With the exception, perhaps, of Izu Peninsula, the Tohoku region, and Hokkaido, driving is not recommended for visitors wishing to tour Japan. Driving is British style (on the left side of the road), which may be hard for those not used to it; traffic can be horrendous; and driving isn't even economical. Not only is gas expensive, but all of Japan's expressways charge high tolls the one-way toll from Tokyo to Kyoto is almost the same price as a ticket to Kyoto on the Shinkansen. And whereas the Shinkansen takes only 3 hours to get to Kyoto, driving can take about 8 hours. In addition, you may encounter few signs in English in remote areas. Driving in cities is even worse: Streets are often hardly wide enough for a rickshaw, let alone a car, and many roads don't have sidewalks so you have to dodge people, bicycles, and telephone poles. Free parking is hard to find, and garages are expensive. Except in remote areas, it just doesn't make sense to drive.

If you're undeterred, a good roundup of more than 800 car-rental agencies in Japan, including those located at airports and train stations, is provided at www2.tocoo.jp, where you can make reservations, see pictures and descriptions of rental cars, and review your knowledge of international traffic signs. Otherwise, major car-rental companies in Japan include Toyota Rent-A-Car (tel. 03/5954-8020 in Tokyo, or 0800/7000-815 toll-free; www.rent.toyota.co.jp); Nippon Rent-A-Car Service (tel. 03/3485-7196 for the English Service Desk; www.nipponrentacar.co.jp), Nissan Rent-A-Car (tel. 0120/00-4123 toll-free), and Avis (tel. 0120/31-1911 toll-free; www.avis-japan.com). In Hokkaido, Kyushu, and some other areas, there is also JR Eki Rent-A-Car, located beside JR train stations and offering 20% discounts on train fares booked in conjunction with car rentals; you can reserve these cars at any JR Travel Service Center (located in train stations) anywhere in Japan.

Rates vary, but the average cost for 24 hours with unlimited mileage is about ¥10,500 for a subcompact including insurance but not gas; in some tourist areas, such as Hokkaido, rates are more expensive in peak season.

If you do intend to drive in Japan, you'll need either an international or a Japanese driving license. Remember, cars are driven on the left side of the road, and signs on all major highways are written in both Japanese and English. It is against the law to drink alcohol and drive, and you must wear seat belts at all times. Be sure to purchase a bilingual map, as back roads often have names of towns written in Japanese only. Recommended is the *Shobunsha Road Atlas Japan*, available in bookstores that sell English-language books; it also contains maps of major cities, including Tokyo, Sapporo, Hiroshima, and others.

Breakdowns & Assistance: The Japan Automobile Federation (JAF;www.jaf.or.jp) is one of several road service providers maintaining emergency telephone boxes along Japan's major arteries to assist drivers whose cars have broken down or drivers who need help. Calls from these telephones are free and will connect you to JAF's operation center at your request. English is spoken.

By Ferry

Because Japan is an island nation, an extensive ferry network links the string of islands. Although travel by ferry takes longer, it's also cheaper and can be a pleasant, relaxing experience. For example, you can take a ferry from Osaka to Beppu (on Kyushu), with fares starting at ¥8,800 for the 11-hour trip. Unfortunately, information in English is hard to come by. Contact the Tourist Information Center for details concerning routes, prices, schedules, and telephone numbers of the various ferry companies.

Advices on Dining

Ordering: The biggest problem facing the hungry foreigner in Japan is ordering a meal in a restaurant without an English-language menu. This guide alleviates the problem to some extent by recommending sample dishes and giving prices for restaurants throughout Japan; we've also noted which restaurants offer English-language menus.

One aid to simplified ordering is the use of plastic food models in glass display cases either outside or just inside the front door of many restaurants, especially those in tourist areas and department stores. Sushi, tempura, daily specials, spaghetti they're all there in mouthwatering plastic replicas along with corresponding prices. Simply decide what you want and point it out to staff.

Unfortunately, not all restaurants in Japan have plastic display cases, especially the more exclusive or traditional ones. In fact, you'd be missing a lot of Japan's best cuisine if you restrict yourself to eating only at places with displays. If there's no display from which to choose, the best thing to do is see whether the Japanese-language menu has photos or to look at what people around you are eating and order what looks best. Or, order the *teishoku,* or daily special meal (also called "set course" or simply "course," especially in restaurants serving Western food); these fixed-price meals consist of a main dish and several side dishes, including soup, rice, and Japanese pickles. Although most restaurants have set courses for dinner as well, lunch is the usual time for the teishoku, generally from 11 or 11:30am to 1:30 or 2pm.

In any case, once you've decided what you want to eat, flag down a waiter or waitress; they will not hover around your table waiting for you to order but come only when summoned. In most restaurants there are no assigned servers to certain tables; rather, servers are multitaskers, so don't be shy about stopping any who pass by.

Hours: In larger cities, most restaurants are open from about 11am to 10 or 11pm. Of course, some establishments close earlier at 9pm, while others stay open past midnight; the majority close for a few hours in the afternoon (2-5pm). In big cities like Tokyo or Osaka, try to avoid the lunchtime rush from noon to 1pm. In rural areas and small towns, restaurants tend to close early, often by 7:30 or 8pm. Traditional Japanese restaurants hang a *noren* (split curtain) over the front door to signify they're open.

Another thing to keep in mind is that the closing time posted for most restaurants is exactly that everyone is expected to pay his or her bill and leave. A general rule of thumb is that the last order is taken at least a half-hour before closing time, sometimes an hour or more for *kaiseki* restaurants (staff will usually alert you they're taking last orders). To be on the safe side, try to arrive at least an hour before closing time so you have time to relax and enjoy your meal.

Taxes: Keep in mind that first-class restaurants will also add a 10% to 15% service charge, as do most hotel restaurants.

Etiquette

Upon Arrival: As soon as you're seated in a Japanese restaurant (that is, a restaurant serving Japanese food), you'll be given a wet towel, which will be steaming hot in winter or pleasantly cool in summer. Called an *oshibori,* it's for wiping your hands. In all but the fancy restaurants, men can get away with wiping their faces as well, but women are not supposed to (I ignore this if it's hot and humid outside). Sadly, some cheaper Japanese restaurants now resort to a paper towel wrapped in plastic, which isn't nearly the same. Oshibori are generally not provided in Western restaurants.

Chopsticks: The next thing you'll probably be confronted with is chopsticks (though knives and forks are used in restaurants serving

Western food). The proper way to use a pair is to place the first chopstick between the base of the thumb and the top of the ring finger (this chopstick remains stationary) and the second one between the top of the thumb and the middle and index fingers. (This second chopstick is the one you move to pick up food.)

The best way to learn to use chopsticks is to have a Japanese person show you how. It's not difficult, but if you find it impossible, some restaurants might have a fork as well. How proficiently foreigners handle chopsticks is a matter of great curiosity for Japanese, and they're surprised if you know how to use them; even if you were to live in Japan for 20 years, you would never stop receiving compliments on how talented you are with chopsticks.

Chopstick Etiquette: If you're taking something from a communal bowl or tray, you're supposed to turn your chopsticks upside down and use the part that hasn't been in your mouth; after transferring the food to your plate, you turn the chopsticks back to their proper position. The exception is *shabu-shabu* and sukiyaki.

Never point at someone with your chopsticks, and never stick them down vertically into your bowl of rice and leave them there, and never pass anything from your chopsticks to another person's chopsticks both actions have origins relating to funerary rites but are now mostly considered bad manners.

Eating Soup & Noodles: You don't use a spoon with Japanese soup. Rather, you'll pick up the bowl and drink from it, using your chopsticks to fish out larger pieces of food. You should also pick up a bowl of rice to eat it. It's considered good taste to slurp with gusto, especially if you're eating hot noodles. Noodle shops in Japan are always well orchestrated with slurps and smacks.

Drinking: Women should hold their glass or cup with both hands, but men do not. If you're drinking in Japan, the main thing to remember is that you never pour your own glass. Bottles of beer are so large that people often share one. The rule is that in turn, one person pours for everyone else in the group, so be sure to hold up your glass when someone is pouring for you. As the night progresses Japanese get sloppy about this rule. It took me awhile to figure this out, but if no one notices your empty glass, the best thing to do is to pour everyone else a drink so that someone will pour yours. If someone wants to pour you a drink and your glass is full, the proper thing to do is to take a few gulps so that he or she can fill your glass. Because each person is continually filling everyone else's glass, you never know exactly how much you've had to drink, which (depending on how you look at it) is either very good or very bad. If you really don't want more to drink, leave your glass full and refuse refills.

Paying the Bill: If you go out with a group of friends (not as a visiting guest of honor and not with business associates), it's customary to split the dinner bill equally, even if you all ordered different things. Even foreigners living in Japan adopt the practice of splitting the bill; it certainly makes figuring everyone's share easier, especially since there's no tipping in Japan. But it can be hard on frugal diners on a budget. If you're with friends who do wish to pay for only what they ate, tell the cashier you want to pay *"betsu, betsu."*

Other Tips: It's considered bad manners to walk down the street eating or drinking (except at a festival). You'll notice that if a Japanese buys a drink from a vending machine, he'll stand there, gulp it down, and throw away the container before going on. To the chagrin of their elders, young Japanese sometimes ignore this rule.

How to Eat Without Spending a Fortune

During your first few days in Japan particularly if you're in Tokyo money will seem to flow from your pockets like water. In fact, money has a tendency to disappear so quickly that many people become convinced they must have lost some of it somehow. At this point, almost everyone panics (I've seen it happen again and again), but with time they slowly realize that because prices are markedly different here (steeper), a bit of readjustment in thinking and habits is necessary. Coffee, for example, is something of a luxury, and some Japanese are astonished at the thought of drinking four cups a day. Here are some tips for getting the most for your yen.

Breakfast: Buffet breakfasts are popular at Japanese hotels and can be an inexpensive way to eat your fill. Otherwise, coffee shops offer what's called "morning service" until 10 or 11am; it generally consists of a cup of coffee, a small salad, a boiled egg, and the thickest slice of toast you've ever seen for about ¥650. That's a real bargain when you consider that just one cup of coffee can cost ¥250 to ¥500. (Except at most hotel breakfast buffets, there's no such thing as the bottomless cup in Japan.) There are many coffee-shop chains in Japan, including Doutour, Pronto, and the ever-expanding Starbucks (854 in Japan at last count).

Set Lunches Eat your biggest meal at lunch: Many restaurants serving Japanese food offer a daily set lunch, or *teishoku,* at a fraction of what their set dinners might be. Usually ranging in price from ¥800 to ¥2,000, they're generally available from about 11am to around 2pm. A Japanese teishoku will include the main course (such as tempura, grilled fish, or the specialty of the house), soup, pickled vegetables, rice, and tea, while the set menu in a Western-style restaurant (often called set lunch) usually consists of a main dish, salad, bread, and coffee.

Cheap Eats: Inexpensive restaurants can be found in department stores (often one whole floor will be devoted to various kinds of restaurants, most with plastic-food displays), underground shopping arcades, nightlife districts, and in and around train and subway stations. Some of the cheapest establishments for a night out on the town are yakitori-ya, izakaya (Japanese pubs), noodle and ramen shops, coffee shops (which often offer inexpensive pastries and sandwiches), and conveyor-belt sushi restaurants where you reach out and take the plates that interest you. Restaurants serving *gyudon* (beef bowl) are also cheap, with Yoshinoya the largest chain. Japan also has American fast-food chains, such as McDonald's (where Big Macs cost about ¥320) and KFC, as well as Japanese chains Freshness Burger and First Kitchen, among them that sell hamburgers.

Ethnic restaurants: particularly those serving Indian, Korean, Chinese, Italian, and other cuisines, are plentiful and usually inexpensive. Hotel restaurants can also be good bargains for inexpensive set lunches or buffets (called *viking* in Japanese), while inexpensive drinking places are good bets for dinner.

Street-side stalls, called yatai, are also good sources of inexpensive meals. These restaurants-on-wheels sell a variety of foods, including *oden* (fish cakes), *yakitori* (skewered barbecued chicken), and *yakisoba* (fried noodles), as well as sake and beer. They appear mostly at night, lighted by a single lantern or a string of lights, and most have a counter with stools as well, protected in winter by a wall of tarp. These can be great, cozy places for rubbing elbows with the locals. Fukuoka, in Kyushu, is famous for its yatai, but you may find them also near other cities' nightlife districts. Sadly, traditional pushcarts are being replaced by motorized vans, which are not nearly as romantic and do not offer seating.

Prepared Foods: You can save even more money by avoiding restaurants altogether. There are all kinds of prepared foods you can buy; some are even complete meals, perfect for picnics in a park or right in your hotel room.

Perhaps the best known is the *obento*, or box lunch, commonly sold on express trains, on train-station platforms, in food sections of department stores, and at counter windows of tiny shops throughout Japan. In fact, the obento served by vendors on trains and at train stations are an inexpensive way to sample regional cuisine since they often include food typical of the region you're passing through.

Costing between ¥800 and ¥1,500, the basic obento contains a piece of meat (generally fish or chicken), various side dishes, rice, and pickled vegetables. Sushi boxed lunches are also readily available.

My favorite place to shop for prepared foods is department stores. Located in basements, these enormous food and produce sections hark back to Japanese markets of yore, with vendors yelling out their wares and crowds of housewives deciding on the evening's dinner. Different counters specialize in different items tempura, *yakitori,* eel, Japanese pickles, cooked fish, sushi (sometimes made by robots!), salads, vegetables, and desserts. Almost the entire spectrum of Japanese cuisine is available, as are numerous samples. There are also counters selling obento box meals. In any case, you can eat for less than ¥1,200, and there's nothing like milling with Japanese housewives to make you feel like one of the locals. Though not as colorful, 24-hour convenience stores and grocery stores also sell packaged foods like sandwiches and obento.

Information for Families

Japanese are very fond of children, which makes traveling in Japan with kids a delight. All social reserve seems to be waived for children. Taking along some small and easy-to-carry gifts (such as colorful stickers) for your kids to give to other children is a great icebreaker.

Safety also makes Japan a good destination for families. Still, plan your itinerary with care. To avoid crowds, visit tourist sights on weekdays. Never travel on city transportation during rush hour or on trains during popular public holidays. And remember that with all the stairways and crowded sidewalks, strollers are less practical than baby backpacks.

Children 6 to 11 years old are generally charged half-price for everything from temple admission to train tickets, while children 5 and under are often admitted free. Tourist spots in Japan almost always have a table or counter with a stamp and inkpad so that visitors can commemorate their trip; you might wish to give your children a small notebook so they can collect imprints of every attraction they visit. There are many attractions throughout Japan geared just toward kids, including sophisticated theme parks. And what teenager could resist Japan's pop culture, fashion, and fads?

Although it's not advertised, many hotels and *ryokan* (Japanese-style inns) give discounts to young children (up to 5 or 9 years of age) or allow them to stay for free, but only if they sleep with you and do not require an extra bed. Ryokan may also give discounts for meals. At budget chain Tokyo Inn, for example, children 5 and under stay free, while those 6 to 10 are charged an extra ¥1,050 per night. In any case, it's advisable to ask in advance. Many upper-range hotels in major cities like Tokyo and Osaka provide babysitting services, although they are prohibitively expensive. Expect to fork over a minimum of ¥5,000 for 2 hours of freedom.

As for food, the transition from kid-favorite spaghetti to *udon* noodles is easy, and udon and *soba* shops are inexpensive and ubiquitous. In addition, most family-style restaurants, especially those in department stores, offer a special children's meal that often includes a small toy or souvenir. For those real emergencies, Western fast-food places such as McDonald's and KFC are seemingly everywhere in Japan.

Escorted & Package Tours

Escorted tours are structured group tours, with a group leader. The price usually includes everything from airfare to hotels, meals, tours, admission costs, and local transportation. They take you to the maximum number of sights in the minimum amount of time with the least amount of hassle. On the downside, you'll have little opportunity for serendipitous interactions with locals. Tours can be jampacked with activities, leaving little room for individual sightseeing, whim, or adventure plus they often focus on heavily touristed sites, missing out on lesser-known gems.

That said, lots of tour companies offer group trips to Japan, including General Tours(tel. 800/221-2216; www.generaltours.com), which offers tours to major tourist destinations in Japan. JTB USA (tel. 800/235-3523; www.jtbusa.com) offers tours that may highlight anything from Japanese cuisine to art. Esprit Travel & Tours (tel. 800/377-7481; www.esprittravel.com) specializes in small-group walking, hiking, and cultural tours that cover such interests as textile arts, Japanese gardens, and the old Tokaido Road. If you want someone else to take care of logistics but don't like group tours, Artisans of Leisure (tel. 800/214-8144; www.artisansofleisure.com) provides luxury tours with private guides that are tailored to your interests. U.K.-based InsideJapan Tours (tel. 0117/314-4620; www.insidejapantours.com) offers small escorted tours to both known destinations and places off the beaten track. If you want to know more about sake, take 5-day Sake Brewery Tour offered by sake expert John Gauntner (tel. 415/5780-4565; www.sake-world.com).

For more ideas on escorted tours departing from North America, go to www.japantravelinfo.com; for tours departing from England, go to www.seejapan.co.uk. For more information on escorted tours, including questions to ask before booking your trip, see www.frommers.com/planning.

Special-Interest Trips

If your primary interest lies with *ikebana* (Japanese flower arranging), the tea ceremony, or other cultural pursuits, Tokyo and Kyoto are your best bets for finding instruction in English. For short introductions, Sunrise Tours (www.jtb-sunrisetours.jp) offers the chance to experience the tea ceremony on 2- or 3-hour tours in both Tokyo and Kyoto, along with other cultural pursuits such as making sushi or writing calligraphy. Tokyo-based H.I.S. Experience Japan (www.hisexperience.jp) offers a wide range of hands-on activities, including a samurai sword class featuring a sword fight demonstration by instructors and a lesson covering the basic movements; a visit to a sumo stable followed by a typical sumo meal; a *taiko* drumming or *shamisen*course; a kimono workshop; a survival Japanese-language class; and cooking classes that cover sushi, *soba,* and traditional Japanese food.

In Tokyo, there are several ikebana schools offering one-time or ongoing instruction in English. In Kyoto, the Women's Association of Kyoto (www.wakjapan.com) offers short, one-time classes on the tea ceremony, flower arranging, origami, Japanese calligraphy, Japanese cooking, and other cultural activities. The tourist offices in both Tokyo and Kyoto have information on temples that provide *zazen* (sitting meditation) in English.

You won't become fluent in Japanese in a week or two, but for longer stays there are language schools in major cities across Japan that cater to both the beginner and the intermediate. Check the classified sections of city magazines, like *Metropolis* in Tokyo, for lists of language schools.

Outside Tokyo and Kyoto, local international centers in larger cities, founded to promote multicultural harmony and to assist foreigners living in their communities, are good resources for cultural activities and events. The Nagoya International Center(www.nic-nagoya.or.jp), for example, offers seven levels of Japanese instruction, from conversation for beginners to writing kanji, at reasonable prices. In Kanazawa, the Ishikawa International Lounge (www.ifie.or.jp) schedules cultural events and classes that might cover origami, calligraphy, the tea ceremony, Japanese flower arranging, Japanese folk dancing, Japanese cooking, and Japanese language; classes themselves are free, but materials for the class cost extra. Other cities with similar institutions, all offering Japanese language classes and sometimes cultural classes as well, include the International House, Osaka (www.ih-osaka.or.jp), Kobe's Hyogo International Association (www.hyogo-ip.or.jp/en), the Okayama Prefectural International Exchange Foundation (www.opief.or.jp/english), and the Hiroshima International Center (www.hiroshima-ic.or.jp).

Gay and Lesbian Travelers

While there are many gay and lesbian establishments in Tokyo (concentrated mostly in Shinjuku's Ni-chome district), the gay community in Japan is not a vocal one, and in any case, local information in English is hard to come by. A useful website for gay club listings is www.utopia-asia.com/tipsjapn.htm, where you can also order the *Utopia Guide to Japan,* which covers the gay and lesbian scene in 27 cities in Japan.

Student Travelers

Students sometimes receive discounts at museums, though occasionally discounts are available only to students enrolled in Japanese schools. Furthermore, discounted prices are often not displayed in English. Your best bet is to bring along an International Student Identity Card (ISIC) together with your university student ID and show them both at ticket windows. For information on the ISIC card and where and how to obtain one, check the
website www.isic.org.

Travelers with Disabilities

For those with disabilities, traveling can be a nightmare in Japan, especially in Tokyo and other large metropolises. City sidewalks can be so jampacked that getting around on crutches or in a wheelchair is exceedingly difficult; some busy thoroughfares can be crossed only via pedestrian bridges.

Most major train and subway stations now have elevators, but they can be difficult to locate. Otherwise, smaller stations, especially in rural areas, may be accessible only by stairs or escalators, though in recent years some have been equipped with powered seat lifts. While some buses are now no-step conveyances for easy access, subway and train compartments are difficult for solo wheelchair travelers to navigate on their own due to a gap or slight height difference between the coaches and platforms. In theory you can ask a station attendant to help you board, though you might have to wait if he's busy; you can also request an attendant at your destination to help you disembark. Although trains and buses have seating for passengers with disabilities called "Priority Seats" and located in the first and last compartments of the train subways can be so crowded that there's barely room to move. Moreover, Priority Seats are almost always occupied by commuters, so unless you look visibly handicapped, no one is likely to offer you a seat.

As for accommodations, only 10% of the nation's hotels have barrier-free rooms (called a "universal" room in Japan and used primarily by seniors), mostly in the expensive category. Only a scant 1% of Japanese inns have such rooms. Lower-priced accommodations may also lack elevators.

Restaurants can also be difficult to navigate, with raised doorsills, crowded dining areas, and tiny bathrooms that cannot accommodate wheelchairs. Best bets for ramps and easily accessible bathrooms include restaurants in department stores and upper-end hotels. Even Japanese homes are not very accessible, since the main floor is always raised about a foot above the entrance-hall floor.

For information on traveling with a wheelchair, including limited information on a handful of sights and hotels offering facilities for travelers with disabilities, visit the Accessible Japan website at www.tesco-premium.co.jp/aj.

When it comes to facilities for the blind, Japan has a very advanced system. At subway stations and on many major sidewalks in large cities, raised dots and lines on the ground guide blind people at intersections and to subway platforms. In some cities, streetlights chime a theme when the signal turns green east-west, and chime another for north-south. Even Japanese yen notes are identified by a slightly raised circle the ¥1,000 note has one circle in a corner, while the ¥10,000 note has two. Many elevators have floors indicated in Braille, and some hotels identify rooms in Braille.

Regions in Brief

Separated from mainland China and Korea by the Sea of Japan, the nation of Japan stretches in an arc about 2,900km (1,800 miles) long from northeast to southwest, yet it is only 403km (250 miles) wide at its broadest point. Japan consists primarily of four main islands Honshu, Hokkaido, Shikoku, and Kyushu. Surrounding these large islands are more than 6,000 smaller, mostly uninhabited islands and islets. Far to the southwest are the Okinawan islands, perhaps best known for the fierce fighting that took place there during World War II and for their continued (and controversial) use as an American military base. If you were to superimpose Japan's four main islands onto a map of the United States, they would stretch all the way from Boston to Atlanta, which should give you an idea of the diversity of Japan's climate, flora, and scenery Hokkaido in the north is subarctic, while Kyushu is subtropical. Honshu, Japan's most populous island and home to Tokyo, Kyoto, and Osaka, is connected to the other three islands by tunnel or bridge, which means you can travel to all four islands by train.

As much as 70% of Japan consists of mountains. They are found on all four main islands and most are volcanic in origin. Altogether, there are some 265 volcanoes, more than 30 of them still considered active. Mount Fuji (on Honshu), dormant since 1707, is Japan's highest and most famous volcano, while Mount Aso (on Kyushu) boasts the largest caldera in the world. Because of its volcanic origins, earthquakes have plagued Japan throughout its history. In the 20th century, the two most destructive earthquakes were the 1923 Great Kanto Earthquake, which killed more than 100,000 people in the Tokyo area, and the 1995 Great Hanshin Earthquake, which claimed more than 6,000 lives in Kobe.

Japan is divided into 47 regional divisions, or prefectures. Each prefecture has its own prefectural capital and is comparable to the U.S. state or the British county, though prefectures vary greatly in size (greater Tokyo is one prefecture; all of Hokkaido is another). Japan's total landmass is slightly smaller than California in area, yet Japan has 41% the population of the United States. And because three-fourths of Japan is mountainous and therefore uninhabitable, its people are concentrated primarily in only 10% of the country's landmass, with the rest of the area devoted to agriculture. In other words, imagine 41% of the U.S. population living in California primarily in San Diego County and you get an idea of how crowded Japan is. For this island nation isolated physically from the rest of the world, struck repeatedly through the centuries by earthquakes, fires, and typhoons, and possessed of only limited space for harmonious living geography and topography have played major roles both in determining its development and in shaping its culture, customs, and arts.

Honshu

Of the four main islands, Honshu is the largest and most populated. Because it's also the most important historically and culturally, it's where most visitors spend the bulk of their time.

Kanto District Located in east-central Honshu and comprising metropolitan **Tokyo** and six prefectures, this district is characterized by the Kanto Plain, the largest flatland in Japan. Although development of the district didn't begin in earnest until the establishment of the shogunate government in Edo (present-day Tokyo) in 1603, Tokyo and surrounding giants such as Yokohama make this the most densely populated region in Japan.

Kansai District Also called the Kinki District and encompassing seven prefectures, this is Japan's most historic region. Nara and Kyoto two of Japan's ancient capitals are here, as are two of Japan's most important port cities, Kobe and Osaka. Since the 1994 opening of Kansai

International Airport outside Osaka, many foreign visitors opt to bypass Tokyo altogether in favor of Kansai's many historic spots, including Mount Koya with its many temples, Himeji with what I consider to be Japan's most beautiful castle, Ise-Shima National Park with Japan's most revered Shinto shrine, Nara with its Great Buddha and temples, and, of course, Kyoto, the former capital for more than 1,000 years with so many temples, imperial villas, and gardens that it ranks as Japan's foremost tourist destination.

Chubu District The Chubu District lies between Tokyo and Kyoto and straddles central Honshu from the Pacific Ocean to the Japan Sea, encompassing nine prefectures. Nagoya, Japan's fourth-largest city and home to an international airport nicknamed Centrair, is Chubu's most important city and a gateway to its other destinations. The district features mountain ranges (including the Japan Alps), volcanoes (including Mount Fuji), large rivers, and coastal regions on both sides of the island. It's popular for skiing and hiking, for quaint mountain villages such as Takayama and Shirakawa-go, and for tourist attractions that include the open-air Museum Meiji Mura (near Nagoya), the castle in Matsumoto, and Kenrokuen Garden in Kanazawa, considered one of Japan's finest.

The Japan Alps Spreading over central Honshu in the Chubu District, the Japan Alps are among Japan's most famous mountain ranges, especially since hosting the 1998 XVIII Winter Olympics in Nagano. Chubu-Sangaku National Park (also called the Japan Alps National Park) contains some of the nation's most beautiful mountain scenery and the country's best skiing, while destinations like Takayama and Shirakawa-go boast quaint historic districts and thatched-roof farmhouses.

Ise-Shima Shima Peninsula, in Mie Prefecture, juts into the Seto Inland Sea and is famous for Ise-Shima National Park, noted for its coastal scenery and Ise Jingu Shrines. Toba, birthplace of the cultured pearl, is popular for its Mikimoto Pearl Island and the Toba Aquarium. Shima Peninsula also boasts two theme parks, one fashioned after Japan's Warring States Era and the other an amusement park with a Spanish theme.

Chugoku District Honshu's western district has five prefectures and is divided by the Chugoku Mountain Range. Industrial giants such as Hiroshima and Okayamalead as the major cities, drawing tourists with reconstructed castles, Korakuen Garden, and the sobering Peace Memorial Park in Hiroshima, dedicated to victims of the world's first atomic bomb. Kurashiki is a must for its photogenic, historic warehouse district, while Miyajima, part of the Seto-Naikai (Inland Sea) National Park, is considered one of Japan's most beautiful islands.

Tohoku District Northeastern Honshu, with Sendai as its regional center, encompasses six prefectures. Known as the Tohoku District, it isn't nearly as developed as the central and southern districts of Honshu, due in large part to its rugged, mountainous terrain and harsh climate. Matsushima, about halfway up the coast between Tokyo and the northern tip of Honshu, is the district's major tourist destination; with its pine-clad islets dotting the bay, it's considered one of Japan's most scenic spots. Kakunodate, located inland, is a former castle town offering preserved samurai houses and, during cherry-blossom season, a stunning show of pink flowers to travelers willing to take a road less traveled. Towada-Hachimantai National Park, which extends over three prefectures, boasts scenic lakes, rustic hot-spring spas, hiking, and skiing.

Hokkaido

Japan's second-largest island, Hokkaido lies to the north of Honshu and is regarded as the country's last frontier with its wide-open pastures, evergreen forests, mountains, gorges, crystal-clear lakes, and wildlife, much of it preserved in national parks. Originally occupied by the indigenous Ainu, it was colonized by Japanese settlers mostly after the Meiji Restoration in 1868. Today it's home to 5.7 million people, 1.9 million of whom live in Sapporo. With a landmass that accounts for 22% of Japan's total area, Hokkaido has the nation's lowest population density: about 4.5% of the total population. That, together with the island's cold, severe winters but mild summers, and its unspoiled natural beauty make this island a nature lover's paradise.

Shikoku

Shikoku, the smallest of the four main islands, is off the beaten path for many foreign visitors. It's famous for its 88 Buddhist temples founded by one of Japan's most interesting historical figures, the Buddhist priest Kukai, known posthumously as Kobo Daishi. Other major attractions are Ritsurin Park in Takamatsu, Matsuyama Castle in Matsuyama, and Dogo Spa, one of Japan's oldest hot-spring spas. For active travelers, the Shimanami Kaido route offers 70 scenic km (43 miles) of dedicated biking trails that connect Shikoku with Hiroshima Prefecture via six islands and a series of bridges in the Seto Inland Sea.

Kyushu

The southernmost of the four main islands, Kyushu boasts a mild subtropical climate, active volcanoes, and hot-spring spas. Because it's the closest major island to Korea and China, Kyushu served as a gateway to the continental mainland throughout much of Japan's history, later becoming the springboard for both traders and Christian missionaries from the West. Fukuoka, Kyushu's largest city, serves as the rail gateway from Honshu, dispersing travelers to hot springs in Beppu, Unzen, and Ibusuki and to such major attractions as Kumamoto Castle in Kumamoto and Sengan-en Garden in Kagoshima. Nagasaki, victim of the world's second atomic bomb, is one of Japan's most cosmopolitan cities.

Okinawa

Okinawa is comprised of 160 islands stretching 400km (248 miles) north to south and 1,000km (620 miles) east to west. Part of the Ryukyu Island chain, Okinawa developed its own languages, culture, cuisine, and architecture under the Ryukyu Kingdom, which traded extensively with both Japan and China before being annexed to Japan after the 1868 Meiji Restoration. Okinawa Island, the largest Ryukyu island, is home to Naha(Okinawa Prefecture's capital), large U.S. military bases, war memorials, and natural attractions, including white sandy beaches and coral reefs popular with divers and snorkelers. Other popular destinations include the laid-back, mostly rural Kume Island and Iriomote Island, 80% of it protected in state and national parks and boasting dense forests, mangroves, and pristine beaches.

Historical Towns

Kurashiki Bikan Historical Quarter

A retro-modern streetscape where you can still feel the presence of people's lives

The town of Kurashiki, Okayama Prefecture, facing the Seto Inland Sea, is one of the largest industrial towns in Western Japan, as well as a sightseeing city that preserves the atmosphere of olden day Japan. Building structures constructed in different eras from the 17th to 20th centuries are preserved without being washed away by the waves of time, to form a retro-modern town that attracts many tourists.

The Kurashiki Bikan Historical Quarter is a symbolic area of the town. Scenery of the old days is still mostly preserved, with white earthen-walled warehouses and villas lined up along Kurashiki River, weeping willows swinging their branches over the river, and stone bridges. Boats carrying supplies used to ply the Kurashiki River, but now sightseeing river boats operate there. You can look up at the streetscape from the river on these boats.

This area is also characteristic in that many people still actually make a living in these buildings. Walk down the alleys to find cafes, souvenir stores and galleries in refurbished warehouses, and merchant's houses-great places to drop in for a break.

nformation

Address: 1 Chuo, Kurashiki City, Okayama

Phone: 086-426-3411 (Sightseeing Department, Culture and Sightseeing Division, Cultural and Industrial Affairs Bureau, Kurashiki City Office)

Hachiman-bori

An artificial channel that supported the growth and prosperity of the castle town as the main artery connecting the town and the largest lake in Japan, Lake Biwa

Hachimanbori is a channel running through the center of Omihachiman City, Shiga Prefecture. In 1585, Toyotomi Hidetsugu, who was the nephew of Toyotomi Hideyoshi (the ruler of Japan at the end of the 16th century), built a castle on Mount Hachiman, and the channel was cut open as part of the development of the castle town. Hachimanbori is 4,750 m long in total and connected to Lake Biwa, which is the largest lake in Japan. Hidetsugu made the ships that navigate Lake Biwa stop by at the port near Hachimanyama Castle to invigorate the flow of people and goods. Hachimanbori had become the main artery that contributed in significantly developing the towns nearby. The town of Omihachiman continued to grow and prosper well after the governance of the Toyotomi Family, as far as until the late Edo Period (1603-1868).

Entering the Showa Period (1929-1989), transportation by water began to diminish with the development of land traffic, and the presence of Hachimanbori also faded. There were even times when the filling of the channel was considered. However, citizens who tried to preserve the precious asset that served as the foundation of the town started preservation and improvement activities. With the efforts of such residents, Hachimanbori gradually regained its beauty. We can still see rows of storehouses and old merchant houses along the channel, showing the remnants of the streetscape of the time when the town prospered. There is also a sightseeing boat cruising Hachimanbori, from which you can enjoy more vivid scenery.

Nagasaki Shinchi Chinatown
One of the three largest Chinatowns in Japan, along with Yokohama and Kobe

Nagasaki Chinatown, located in Nagasaki City, Nagasaki Prefecture, is one of the three largest Chinatowns in Japan, along with the Chinatowns in Yokohama and Kobe. Even during the Edo Period (1603-1868), when national isolation was the basic national policy, Nagasaki was opened as an exception for trade with China. At its peak, it is said that there were about 10,000 Chinese residents in Nagasaki City, mainly those from Fujian. However, Chinese houses thereafter became confined to the hills for a long time. After the Chinese houses were abandoned with the opening of Japan to foreign countries in 1859, the Chinese residents in Nagasaki transferred to Shinchi Town. Thus, a Chinatown was formed, gradually developing into the current unique sightseeing spot with about 40 stores, including Chinese restaurants, confectionery stores, and China-made souvenir stores.

The vermilion-lacquered Chinese gates in each of the four sides of Chinatown were constructed by craftsmen and materials from Fuzhou, China, with a wish to develop into a Chinatown comparable to those of Yokohama and Kobe. The notable characteristic of the gates is that they carry the sculpture of the god of the four directions, that is, Azure Dragon for the east gate, White Tiger for the west gate, Vermilion Bird for the south gate, and Black Tortoise for the north gate. The Nagasaki Lantern Festival is held in the town every February. Although it had originally been a festival for the residents of the Chinatown celebrating the Chinese New Year, the colorful lantern decorations gradually gained a reputation and spread to regions outside of Chinatown as well. Now there are as many as 15,000 Chinese lanterns decorating the streets, attracting tourists from throughout the country.

Tensha-en Garden

An array of hues reflected in the water provide an air of elegant simplicity in this garden formerly belonging to a feudal lord

Overlooking the sea, Uwajima is one of Shikoku's main port towns, which has flourished since the days of yore thanks to its temperate climate and abundant natural resources. Tenshaen is a pond-stroll garden created in 1866, during the final years of the Edo period (1603-1868), as a retreat for Munetada, the seventh feudal lord of the Date clan, which governed this region. It was created in a corner of the Hamagoten residence, which the second lord, Munetoshi, built on land reclaimed from the sea. As the name suggests, a pond-stroll garden is a type of Japanese garden laid out with a large pond at its main focus, with a path around it that enables those walking along it to enjoy views of small islands, bridges, rocks, shrubs, and flowers as they stroll. The name of the garden is taken from a line in a Chinese poem composed by Munetada's ancestor, the warrior Date Masamune.

Visitors to Tenshaen can enjoy the beautiful hues of its flowers: in April, the wisteria on the trellis in the shape of an arched bridge across the pond is a riot of cascading blossom, while in May, about 2,000 irises reach full bloom. In particular, 19 types of bamboo have been planted around the pond , as bamboo and sparrows feature in the kamon crest of the Date clan, creating splendid scenery with an appeal unique to this garden.

Moreover, some of the rocks laid out in the garden are valuable, and even if you are not a particular devotee of Japanese gardens, you won't be able to take your eyes off such rocks as the Roaring Tiger Rock, so named because of its resemblance to a tiger, the Standing Cow and Recumbent Cow rocks, which have a somewhat bovine appearance, and the Sea Rock, which was used for mooring boats. There are many things to see that will make your walk a most rewarding experience.

Mimitsu area

A wondrous townscape featuring remnants of the Edo period, created by the irony of history

The Mimi River flows through the city of Hyuga in Miyazaki Prefecture. The historic port town of Mimitsu lies at its mouth. Today, it is a tranquil and atmospheric port town, but about 150 years ago, it was a prosperous commercial port that was a hub for trade with the cities of Kyoto, Osaka, and Kobe, with so many houses belonging to merchants and shipping agents crowded together that people used to refer to the thousand houses of Mimitsu (Mimitsu-sengen). However, during the Taisho period (1912-1926), as transport switched to railways and roads, the once-bustling port town of Mimitsu suddenly fell into decline, with only its townscape to remind people of its former status.

Nevertheless, in 1986, it was designated as an important preservation district for groups of historic buildings, due to its townscape with remnants of its glory days. Following its sudden return to prominence, in 2007 it was selected as one of Japan's 100 most beautiful historic landscapes and began to attract many visitors.

Among the buildings that line its three main streets running parallel to the sea, Uemachi, Nakamachi, and Shinmachi are picturesque machiya-style townhouses that incorporate many aspects of the architectural style typical of Kyoto and Osaka, such as mushikomado finely-latticed top-floor windows, kyogoshi latticed windows, and white lime plaster walls, all of which are eyecatching in their beauty. In addition, a building that was formerly the premises of a shipping agent, called Kawachiya, has been designated as a cultural asset by the city government and now houses the Hyuga City History and Folk Museum. Visitors to this district, which is almost without parallel in Japan, can conjure up images of what it must have looked like when it was a bustling port town crowded with townhouses, back in the Edo period (1603-1868).

Harimaya-bashi Bridge

Well known as mentioned in big hit song
Cute red arched bridge

Harimaya-bashi is a tiny, 20-meter red arched bridge in an area with department stores and other buildings standing side by side in the heart of Kochi City. The bridge is said to have been given the name because two shops, Harimaya and Hitsuya which stood across the Hori River during the Edo period (1603 to 1868), built a bridge over it for smooth traffic between them. Originally a simple wooden bridge, it was repeatedly torn down and rebuilt, while the river was filled. Through twists and turns, the location has been built into a park with an artificially gully reviving the murmur of a stream.

An old local fork song, Yosakoi, has a phrase of Buddhist priest Junshin buying a hairpin at the bridge for his sweetheart Ouma. A song with the title of "Nangoku Tosa wo Atonishite" made based on the phrase and sung by Peggy Hayama, sold millions of records in the 1960s. The song was also cinemized, prompting tourists to flock to the Harimaya-bashi show in the movie and making the bridge into a sightseeing spot. A monument depicting Junshin and Ouma stands at the foot of the bridge.

Area of traditional warehouses

A town where you can enjoy the contrast of red tiles and white plaster walls at your own pace

The white-walled warehouses can be found near the Tama River in Kurayoshi City, in central Tottori Prefecture. Most of the warehouses were built between the Edo Period (1603-1868) and the Meiji Period (1868-1912). Yakisugi, which are burnt and carbonized cedar boards, have been used for the exterior walls of the warehouses. Many warehouses are lined up on the street for about 400 m along the Tama River. Also, there are merchant houses with red, cold-resistant roof tiles preserved along Hon-cho Street. The red-tiled buildings, numbered from 1 to 16, have been renovated into cafes and galleries while maintaining the appearances they had when they were used for soy sauce making and sake brewing. The scenery of the good old days in Japan can be experienced as you stroll the streets, while shopping, eating and drinking can be enjoyedinside the buildings.

One of the reasons this place is strongly recommended is that although it is well known as a historical town of earthen-walled warehouses, the place is not overcrowded with tourists. You can enjoy the beautiful scenery made of white walls, black boards, and red roofs to your heart's content at a comfortable pace.

Nagamachi Buke Yashiki District

Different appearances catch the eyes of tourists in each season. Kenroku-en Garden and Nagamachi are two popular spots that represent the old city of Kanazawa.

Kanazawa is an old city situated in Ishikawa Prefecture and is the largest city in the Hokuriku region. In the Edo Period, the city prospered as a Kaga domain's castle town with an income rating of over one million 'koku' (unit of measurement to assess wealth), which was the highest in the nation after the shogunate itself. Kanazawa continued to develop as a big city, following Edo (current Tokyo), Osaka, and Kyoto, and since it escaped damage in WWII, there still remains a historic atmosphere throughout its urban area.

One of the spots you will want to visit in the city is a huge Japanese garden, Kenroku-en, which is one of the three great gardens in Japan. Kenroku-en, which means "the garden that combines six attributes," is said to be so named because it miraculously holds six elements that should conflict if existing in one garden: "spaciousness and seclusion," "artifice and antiquity," and "waterways and panoramas." The garden was shaped for a period of over 100 years through several generations of the Kaga domain's lords. It is composed of many ponds, winding streams connecting these ponds, mounds made of turned soil, various trees, and tea houses at spots throughout the garden. Because visitors can enjoy seeing around the garden while dropping in at these spots, this type of garden is called "a strolling garden," and Kenroku-en is a typical example.

If you want to fully enjoy Kenroku-en Garden, you will need to walk for about 90 minutes and 1,300 meters. There are already many beautiful spots that make you stop strolling and see each of them in the garden; however, you will have even more to see in other seasons offering different views, especially in winter. In order to protect the branches of pine trees from heavy snow, a pole is set up and holds up the branches of trees with ropes. This is called "Yukitsuri," and together with the views of lanterns covered with snow, it is a common sight in the garden in winter months. In spring, the garden is filled with pink cherry blossoms, while it is colored by fresh greenery in summer and covered by red leaves in autumn.

Another spot you should not skip is the Nagamachi Samurai Residences District, which still preserves old earthen walls and 'nagaya-mon,' a gate of tenements. Once you step into the backstreets of Korinbo, the central area of Kanazawa City with modern buildings, you will find the district making you feel as if you slipped back to the Edo Period. It was a residential area for middle- and upper-class samurais and still keeps its traditional atmosphere today with earthen walls and stone pavement along with the Onosho Canal.

Surrounded by the earthen walls that continue several hundred meters, as well as the sound of water flowing by the samurai houses and old stone pavements, you can surely feel the history and tradition of this old castle town. In addition, you can see a part of samurai life at the remains of the Kaga domain's Takada family's house or that of the Nomura family, which still retains vestiges of those old days in its garden. Rest houses and tea houses, as well as temples, are also there for your pleasant strolling.

People still live in these houses. Among them, the Nomura family house is open to public, allowing visitors to see the garden and tea house of Nomura Denbei Nobusada, whose income rating was 1,200 koku. The garden of the Takada family is a beautiful strolling garden with a pond that still retains vestiges of the Edo Period. Because of its wonderful sights, the area is often used as a location for filming TV dramas

Hanamaki Area

Hanamaki-onsen-kyo Village provides visitors with attractive, comfortable accommodations and relaxing hot springs.
Hanamaki City, located in the center of the Kitakami Basin in the mid-western part of Iwate Prefecture, is a city of parks centered on hot

spring zones dotted along the Dai-gawa River, a tributary of the Kitakami-gawa River, and the valley of Yunosawa.

Around a dozen hot springs, beginning with the Hanamaki-onsen Hot Spring and including Dai, Shidodaira, Osawa, and Namari, are known collectively as the Hanamaki-onsen-kyo Village which has many different types of accommodation and is a favorite spot for tourists in the Tohoku region (the northeastern region). There are Iwate Hanamaki Airport, providing the only air access to Iwate Prefecture, and Shin-Hanamaki Station on the Tohoku Shinkansen Line. Together they form the gateway to Iwate Prefecture.

Hanamaki is also known as the home of fable writer Kenji Miyazawa, who was born here at the beginning of the 20th century. Kenji's large number of poems and fables are enjoyed by many readers even today for the fresh use of language, unrestrained imagination, and deep social insight. In Hanamaki, there are many places that appear in Miyazawa's fables, including his parents' house, the Miyazawa Kenji Memorial Museum, Kenji Miyazawa Dowa Mura (the village of fables), Poran-no-hiroba Square, and the IHATOV Center. These places attract visitors all year round.

Imabari/Ozu Area

Enjoy the fantastic sceneries of "the Aegean Sea of Orient" connected by magnificent bridges. Try cycling on the sea feeling the breeze.

Shimanami-Kaido (Shimanami Sea Route) is a collective name of the 60 km (37 mile) motor highway over the Seto Inland Sea which connects Imabari City, Ehime Prefecture, and Onomichi City , Hiroshima Prefecture, and six islands in between. The completion of the route has made Ehime more easily accessible from major cities in Honshu. "Shimanami-Kaido" often refers the whole area along the road.

Shimanami-Kaido provides the marvelous views with its splendid bridges. Kurushima-Kaikyo Bridges (4015 m / 13173 ft), which links Oshima Island to Shikoku, are the first three consecutive suspension bridges in the world. To overlook the bridges, the best is Mt. Kiro-san Observatory and Park in Oshima, especially in the sunset. Tatara Bridge (1480 m / 4856 ft), one of the world's longest cable-stayed bridges, spreads its wings over the border of Ehime and Hiroshima. You can enjoy its great view from Tatara Shimanami Park at the foot of the bridge on Omishima Island.

Cycling is the highlight attraction. It is the best recommended cycling course in Japan. Each bridge has the path for pedestrians & cyclers beside the vehicle traffic, which enables you to bike on the bridges between the blue sky and blue sea. There are 14 rent-a-bike stations along the route, where you can take your bike. You may just go around for a while, or you can run as far as you want, and drop off your rental bike at one of the stations. The entire distance of cycling route is approximately 70 km (44 mile), longer than the vehicle highway. It takes less than seven hours.

You may drop in Oyamazumi Shrine on Omishima Island in the center of this area, which has been broadly worshiped since ancient times. It is also famous for the armors and swords the shrine owns, many of which are designated as national treasures and important cultural properties. Tidal current cruises are another recommendation. The islands are dotted closely along the Shimanami-Kaido, which causes strong and complicated tide flow in spots. One of them, Kurushima Kaikyo Strait is known as one of three fastest currents in Japan. The boat-tour takes you to see the dynamic tidal current, the magnificent Kurushima-Kaikyo Bridges and vessels at the shipbuilding docks. You can also enjoy a thrilling cruise to experience on the wildly fast stream at Miyakubo Seto.

Yuya/Asuke Area

Mountain hot springs found along the Chuma-kaido street. An attractive, old fashioned, quaint and authentic townscape.

Yuya is a hot spring resort along the Ure-gawa River in eastern Aichi. In the neighboring areas there is Uma-no-se-iwa, or horseback rocks, designated as a national precious natural monument, where a dyke of andesite rises up in the center of the river, and the precipitous Horai Valley and Mt. Horai-ji-san, where Japanese scops owls live.

Asuke is located in northeastern Aichi. It thrived as a mercantile emporium on the Chuma-kaido street, the route for transporting salt produced along Mikawa Bay in the 19th century. The townscape is plastered with houses along the street reminiscent of the past. There is the "Sanshu Asuke Yashiki", a replica of the townscape in the early 20th century. Here, you can watch performances by the blacksmith, charcoal maker, paper maker, and other artisans inside re-constructed buildings.

Korankei Valley is the most famous spot for fall foliage in Aichi. There are about 4,000 maple trees along the Tomoe-gawa River. The breathtaking beauty of the site is worth seeing. Kojaku-ji Temple, built in 1,427, adds the authentic atmosphere to the whole magnificent scenery.

Sanshu Asuke Yashiki

Look, eat, make: Experience the lifestyle of yesteryear

Until about 50 years ago, the spirit of monodzukuri, the Japanese art of manufacturing, was alive and well in Japanese daily life. People made the things they needed themselves. Today, everything is done for us by machines and we no longer have to use our hands to make things, but this makes life dull and uninteresting. It is this feeling that inspired the opening of Sanshu Asuke Yashiki, which recreates the disappearing Japanese lifestyle of yesteryear and endeavors to pass on handicraft techniques to future generations. With regard to the derivation of the name, Sanshu-meaning Three Rivers-was the name of this area in olden times, and the town in which it is located is Asuke.

When you set foot through the gate, it's like you've instantly taken a step back in time, traveling back about a century. In the garden is a well and a water wheel, with a cow tethered to a post and chickens running around freely. Inside the traditional-style house, you can get a close-up view of artisans demonstrating an array of handicrafts and manual work once carried out in this area, including charcoal-making, paper-making, and weaving. Naturally, visitors can also have a go at some of these crafts themselves, so why not give it a try?

When you get hungry, take a break at Hinoki-chaya, where you can taste the fresh bounty of the mountains, Kunputei, where you can try handmade tofu, or Katakago cafe, which boasts delicious coffee made from beans roasted using charcoal produced here at Sanshu Asuke Yashiki. As time slips slowly by, you'll be enveloped in a tremendous sense of warmth and nostalgia for the good old days

Arita

Town boasting 400-year-hitory of traditional craft
Natural beauty of mountains and forests

Arita is a town located in the southern part of Saga Prefecture and known for Arita porcelain. About 400 years ago, Yi Sam-pyeong, an immigrant Korean potter, and others discovered kaolin in Izumiyama in the town of Arita and began producing porcelain for the first time in Japan.

The Saga feudal domain, which was ruling the area, established a full-scale porcelain production system which contributed to the great development of Arita. The Uchiyama district has developed into a streetscape said to consist of 1,000 kilns and there remain many historically important structures such as houses for lacquer work and Western-style mansions. Many "Tombai" red brick walls, made by plastering scrapped bricks for climbing kilns and porcelain shards with reddish soil, are seen on back streets from quarries in Uchiyama to the Arita Porcelain Museum, creating a well-known streetscape unique to a porcelain town.

Arita is also a town rich in nature as mountains and forests occupy more than 70% of its gross area. There are many beautiful landscapes such as terraced rice paddies on mountain slopes, known as "Tate no Tanada," the pure "Ryumon-kyo" valley, and Mt. Kurokami-zan abounding in rare plants. Visitors to the town can enjoy both traditional craft and rich natural surroundings.

Arita/Imari Area

Arita is the undisputed cradle of porcelain manufacturing. Imari is an intermediary for east and west exchange.

Arita, the cradle of porcelain manufacturing in Japan, is a quiet town among mountains, located in the western part of Saga. Ri Sampei (Korean name, Lee Cham-Pyung), a potter from Korea, discovered a fine-quality white porcelain mineral in Mt. Arita-Izumi-yama. This was the beginning of Arita's development into an internationally known town of porcelain. A monument in memory of Ri Sampei stands in Toyama-jinja Shrine, Arita's chief tutelary shrine.

White-walled houses originating in the 1930s and old Western-style buildings are still present in the Uchiyama area, where many potters once lived. At the back of these buildings, there are Tonbai fences made of used fireproof bricks and old-fashioned potteries. Pottery and porcelain lovers must visit the Kyushu Ceramic Museum and the Arita Ceramic Art Museum in town, where they can see exquisite pottery and porcelain pieces.

Imari, located on the coast of Imari Bay lying between the Higashi Matsu-ura-hanto Peninsula and the Kita Matsu-ura-hanto Peninsula, is a fine natural port and was once an intermediary for the east-west exchange of porcelain. Remnants of the good old days still exist in O-kawachiyama, a secluded pottery center in the mountains. In the 17th and 18th centuries, top-quality gift pieces for the Imperial Court and Shoguns were manufactured there. Accordingly, the porcelain manufacturing method and potters were under very strict management.

Tono-machi

Scenery with vivid carp swimming in roadside canals in this town that produced many well-known personalities

Tonomachi is in Tsuwano Town, Kanoashi County, Shimane Prefecture. Tsuwano is a small castle town located on the border between Shimane and Yamaguchi Prefectures, with a population less than 10,000. Blessed with the abundant nature of the Chugoku Mountains, traditional culture is thriving in this castle town with a history of more than 700 years. It is also referred to as the "Small Kyoto of San-in Region."

Tonomachi is about a ten-minute walk from Tsuwano Station, and is the center of Tsuwano tourism, with old samurai houses, tradesmen's houses, and historical sites. The former Yoro-Kan, where the cultural education and human resource development of Tsuwano Domain took place in the form of academic and military art studies by the masters and pupils of the official samurai of the Domain, is now the Tsuwano Town History Museum, exhibiting various materials. It is said that Mori Ogai, a great writer in the Meiji Period who was born in Tsuwano, studied in Yoro-Kan when he was a child.

There is also the Tago Karo-Mon, which was the former town hall, preserving its grand appearance with a tiled roof. In the roadside canals facing the earthen wall vividly-colored carp swim, and iris flowers bloom in June, which makes for a pleasant sight. The canals are illuminated on summer nights. You can enjoy the beauty in the pleasant cool air at night. It is an atmosphere that can be felt only in small towns.

Tsuwano Area

Affectionately referred to as "Little Kyoto." A castle town with an abundance of nature and historic areas.

Tsuwano is located in the westernmost part of Shimane Prefecture. It is a castle town, developed along the Tsuwano-gawa River and surrounded by nature, and is also called "Little Kyoto" in the San-in region (the Japan Sea Coast). Near Tono-machi in the center of the town, there are streets lined with neat rows of stores and houses, including Sake (rice wine) breweries with lattice doors and Japanese sweets stores, and also samurai residences and storehouses with white plaster walls remaining as they were in the 17th century.

You can find koi, carps of various colors swimming in the waterways along the streets in Tono-machi. The carps in Tsuwano were first kept in the waterways built for irrigation and fire prevention, as emergency provisions in case of famine, in the period from the 17th century to the 19th century.

A holy ritual, horseback archery yabusame is dedicated to the god at Washibara-hachiman-gu Shrine in spring, and together with the heron dance sagimai at Yasaka-jinja Shrine in summer, attract lots of tourists. In addition, Youmei-ji Temple where successive rulers rest and Taikodani-Inari-jinja Shrine where thousands of torii (shrine gates) stand in rows, are some of the well-known tourist sights.

Rosan-do

Tea house where a local lord at the end of Edo Eriod (1853-1868) developed secret plans to bring down the Shogunate

The building is in Kozan-koen Park developed around Ruriko-ji Temple that is a National Treasure. In the park there are a number of historic buildings related to Meiji Restoration (successive reforms to establish a new imperial system.)

At the end of Edo period (1603-1868) called Bakumatsu (1853-1868), there were political movements to bring down Edo Shogunate (Japan had been governed by warrior class and Tokugawa family controlled the government based in Edo Castle) and establish a new government. Mori Motochika, the domain lord at the time, moved the capital to Yamaguchi and built a tea house at the foot of Mount Ichiro (in the present prefectural government.) Under the disguise of tea ceremony, the lord and his subordinate warriors secretly discussed overthrowing of the Edo government. In 1891 after the Meiji Restoration, the tea house that is the present Rosan-do was moved to the current location.

The Kozan-koen Park is dotted with remnants such as Chinryu-tei and Rosan-do from the days of the Meiji Restoration that was the transition stage to modern government, arousing interest in the modern history of Japan. The 5-story pagoda of Ruriko-ji in the park was built during Muromachi period and the symbol of sightseeing in Yamaguchi. The pagoda is illuminated for several hours after sunset. The park is also famous for cherry and plum blossoms attracting a large number of visitors in early spring.

Yamaguchi

An ancient city called the "Kyoto of the West." Dotted with temples and shrines designated as important cultural properties.

Yamaguchi City is located nearly in the center of Yamaguchi Prefecture, and is the center of the local administration. Built in the middle of the 14th century by a warlord in the Ouchi family in imitation of Kyoto, then the capital of Japan, the city was called the "Kyoto of the West" and it prospered.

The five-storied pagoda of Ruriko-ji Temple in Kozan-koen Park, a 31.2-meter-tall national treasure built in the 15th century, is a reflection of the Kyoto culture adopted by the warlord Ouchi. Yasaka-jinja Shrine was erected in the 14th century as a branch of Yasaka-jinja Shrine in Kyoto and relocated to where it is now in the middle of the 19th century. The Yamaguchi Gion-matsuri Festival, modeled after the Gion-matsuri Festival in Kyoto, is staged at the shrine every summer, and the Sagimai Shinji (a ritual heron dance) is dedicated to the shrine.

Also in Kozan-koen Park are historic buildings like the Rosan-do, a bower built for the Mori family that ruled this area in the middle of the 19th century, and the 'uguisu-bari,' the "singing" stone pavement that emits sounds when walked upon that echo throughout the whole neighborhood. Next to the park is Toshun-ji Temple where the graves of the Mori family are located.

Ima-Hachiman-gu Shrine, said to be an ancient shrine already in existence before the Ouchi family arrived to rule Yamaguchi, features the architectural style peculiar to the Yamaguchi region with the entrance gate, front shrine and main shrine all standing in a straight line. It is designated as an important cultural property of Japan.

Youkaichi Gokoku Streetscape Preservation Center

Streetscape of traditional Japanese-style houses, like a scene straight out of a movie

In the 18th century, the major industry of Uchiko Town, Ehime Prefecture, was the production of Japanese wax that was extracted plentifully from Japanese wax trees. There was a high demand for Japanese wax, not only for candles, but also as a glossing agent or ingredient for ointment. The town flourished greatly, and the merchants had built high-quality, handsome houses as if competing with each other.

Entering the era of petroleum in the 19th century, Japanese wax became unnecessary and the handlers have disappeared one after another. However, their beautiful houses remained, fortunately with no major fires. In 1982, the Youkaichi Gokoku district in Uchiko Town was selected as a Group of Traditional Buildings by the national government, and the beauty and high value of the traditional buildings became well known throughout the country.

The characteristic of the streetscape, extending for 600m from north to south along the road, is the architectural style called Hirairi Zukuri, with the walls painted in pale yellows and with lime plaster. Each house is decorated with traditional designs for a Japanese house, including namako walls, gables, plaster reliefs, and tiles on roof ridges, catching visitors' eyes. The narrow alleys between houses also show an original beauty that cannot be found in other places.

The streetscape is the treasure of the town, and the base for its preservation is the Youkaichi Gokoku Streetscape Preservation Center. There are exhibits on the structure of the buildings and tools used for construction, which can be observed free of charge.

Uchiko

A little town remaining fine old homes and warehouses. Strolling along the antique street takes you to the good old days.

Uchiko, a little town within one hour's drive from Matsuyama, flourished from 1720s to 1930s, as a production center for traditional wax made from a kind of nuts, whose quality was worldly recognized. "Yokaichi & Gokoku Quarters", or antique district of those days was designated as an important preservation district for historic buildings. You can stroll the 600 meter long street with fine white and yellowish walled merchants' homes and warehouses, feeling back to its good old days.

Hon-Haga Residence, a dwelling of the Haga family, the most prosperous merchant of the wax production and export, is the most gorgeous building among the district. As the family still lives in this important cultural property house, allowed seeing only the appearance and its garden, the splendid and delicate decorations are worth a look. Another Haga's house, Kami-Haga Residence has a small wax museum, where you can understand how people made good quality whitened wax. Also you should not miss a Japanese candle shop along the street, which is the only one of hand-made candle in a traditional manner. You may watch the master make candles by layering the liquid vegetable wax on the wick.

The wealth by the wax production generated another cultural asset in Uchiko. Uchiko-za Theater, a full-scale theater for Kabuki & Bunraku, was costructed in 1916 by Uchiko merchants, celebrating the Emperor Taisho's coronation. The theater, in ten minutes walk from the classical street, offered the entertainments for local people of those days. After remodeled for other uses, it was restored to original state in 1985. A self-guided tour is available.

Sanno-machi Historic District

A quaint streetscape lined with old merchant houses

Takayama City, Gifu Prefecture, which is roughly in the center of the Japanese archipelago, is a beautiful castle town surrounded by mountains in every direction. It developed as a merchant town nurturing a unique culture in the 1600s, during the Edo Period. The Old Town, consisting of three rows of buildings, is also referred to as "small Kyoto in Hida" due to its quaint atmosphere. It is awarded three stars in the Michelin Travel Guide.

Canals flow under the eaves of merchant houses with latticed bay windows, and there are rows of large warehouses at the back.

Entrances to sake brewing houses are decorated with a ball of cedar leaves to show that the season's new sake is available, recreating the atmosphere of a time when the place was a castle town.

On the banks of Miyagawa River and in the plaza in front of the jinya near the Old Town (Takayama Jinya was the building in which the regional administration was carried out during the Edo Period (1603-1868) and is the only remaining Edo-period jinya in Japan), a morning market opens every day from 6:00 am till around noon. There are various products on sale, including fresh vegetables, fruits, and folk-art products. This is one of the few morning markets in Japan that open 365 days a year, and it is a popular tourist spot. Takayama Festival is the main event of the city, and it is held in spring and fall. It is one of the three most beautiful festivals in Japan, and the city is crowded with many tourists during the festival period.

Takayama Area

A picturesque town with one of the three most beautiful festivals in Japan.

Takayama is located in northern Gifu Prefecture. It is most famous for the Sanno-machi Historic District and the biannual Takayama Festival, which has been designated as one of Japan's most beautiful festivals. During the festival, intricately crafted festival floats are displayed in the city. The floats themselves are testament to the region's history and are a chance to see the culmination of hundred's of years worth of artistry and craftsmanship. The Takayama Festival is held in the spring and fall every year and is attended by thousands of visitors from all over Japan and the world.

Takayama Jinya is a historic government house that was built by the central government in the 17th century. It is the only remaining office of its kind in Japan and is open for tours daily.

Hida Takayama Matsuri no Mori and the Yatai Kaikan are two recommended museums that visitors interested in the Takayama Festival and local artistry are sure to enjoy.

Images of life on farming villages in the Hida region are on display at the Hida Folk Museum (Minzoku-kan).

Hida no Sato is an outdoor museum that displays traditional architecture and thatched roof-houses, some of which have been relocated from the UNESCO World Heritage Site Shirakawa-go.

Every morning a farmer's market is held along the Miya River and in front of Takayama Jinya. Local farmers and craftsmen sell everything from vegetables and pickles to carvings and clothes.

There are many skiing resorts in the Takayama area, which are open during the winter months. The nearby mountains, such as Mt. Norikura are popular for sightseeing and trekking. Additionally the World Heritage Site Shirakawa-go is just a 50 minute bus ride away

Historic Battlefield of Nagakute

Admirable enthusiasm of townspeople trying to preserve historic sites

Japan in the late 1500s was in the Sengoku Era. Warlords around the country were fighting one another to expand their domain. Among them, Oda Nobunaga had risen, aiming to dominate the whole country. However, he was killed in a rebellion by his subordinate on the verge of accomplishing his goal.

The race for his successor reached a peak in 1584, when Toyotomi Hideyoshi, who conquered the country, and Tokugawa Ieyasu, who later became the founder of the Edo Shogunate, fought one another directly in the Battle of Komaki and Nagakute. The story of these great warlords—who led the country thereafter—fighting one another has been handed down as a dramatic event in history.

The battle took place in what is now Nagakute City, near Nagoya City, and the graves of fallen warlords and many other historic sites related to the battle are all neatly preserved here. The site of the major battlefield is developed as Kosenjo Park and is registered as a designated cultural property. Nagakute History Resource Center in the park exhibits a diorama of the battle, armor, helmets, matchlock guns, and other materials. Nagakute Kosenjo Station, located near the park, is a station on the magnetic levitation train line, called "Linimo."

Seto/Nagakute Area

Experiencing the traditional pottery technology, and learn about automobile history at the TOYOTA Automobile Museum.

The City of Seto is famous for its ceramics, which are called 'Setomono' in Japanese, named after the city. The city promotes the movement called "Seto marutto Museum" (the whole town is one gigantic museum). At Kamagaki-no-komichi, a walking path located at the foot of the mountains, plates and cups are embedded in the stone walls of the walkways, and you can gain a sense of the everyday life of the craftspeople.

If you would like to learn about ceramics, we recommend a visit to the Seto Municipal Center of Multimedia and Traditional Ceramics. The traditional-style workshop reproduced here provides an opportunity to observe the work up close. You can also observe or experience crafts such as glass art at the Seto Ceramics and Glass Art Center.

Kamagami-jinja Shrine is rather unusual; it is dedicated to the people who have passed on ceramic manufacturing methods, and the Ceramics Festival is held on the 2nd Saturday and Sunday in September. The kiln-shaped shrine pavilion is quite unique. In the distance, you can see the "Grand Canyon of Seto," a pit from which clay and stone are dug for use in ceramics. Many facilities offer ceramics-making activities, so it is a fun place to visit as a family. The Seto City Tourist Association provides a guide service with English-speaking volunteers.

In Nagakute town, visit "the TOYOTA Automobile Museum", run by TOYOTA Motor Corporation. There are about 120 automobiles from the end of the 19th century to the 1940s including European and American cars.

In the main pavilion, the first automobile produced in Japan is exhibited. You can learn the history of the automobile industry as well as the development of other related technologies. You may find your favorite model in the exhibits.

Hita Area

Hita prospered as Tenryo (direct controlled territory of Edo Shogunate) during the Edo period (1603-1868). It is called "Little

Kyoto", and has old buildings standing in a row, even today, near the hot spring resort. In Mameta town, you can enjoy a stroll through the historic streets.

And Hita is a town that has been blessed with plentiful water for a long time, and is called "Suikyo" (riverside district). Each of the hot spring inns located around the bank of Mikuma River gives a variety of unique ideas. Visitors at the hot spring can enjoy dinner on a leisure boat and atch cormorant fishing in summer.

Hita hot spring is known as "spring for birth", and is effective for neuralgia, recovering from fatigue and more. Many ryokans (Japanese-style inns) in Hita rent out yukata (Japanese summer kimonos) and geta (Japanese sandals) to female guests. This service is very popular because you can choose from among various colors and prints.

Kunisaki-hanto Peninsula Area

An ancient center of Buddhist culture. Rugged, deep ravines extend radially throughout the entire scenic region.

Projecting between the Suo-nada Sea in the Seto Inland Sea and the Iyo-nada Sea, the Kunisaki-hanto Peninsula is formed of large conical volcanoes including 731 m-high Mt. Futago in a northeastern part of Oita. Twenty-eight ravines extend radially with many strangely shaped rocks and stones along them. Ancient Buddhist culture came to stay here, and Buddhist culture unique to this peninsula developed. Many temples and Buddhist remains are scattered all over the peninsula.

In the huge premises, about 150,000 km2 in area, of the Usa-jingu Shrine, which is the head shrine for all Hachimangu Shrines throughout Japan, Uemiya, Shimomiya and other buildings are positioned in an orderly arrangement. The Hatsusawa-ike Pond filled with clean water is located along the front approach beyond the divine bridge.

This center of Buddhist culture boasts many Buddhist National Treasures and Important Cultural Properties such as a wooden figure of Amida-nyorai (Amitabha Tathagata) and wall paintings in colors in the Fuki-ji Temple, statues of Shitenno, the Four Deva Kings in Maki-Odo and a figure of Fudo, the god of fire, known as "Kumano-magai-butsu". Exhibits related to the history and culture of Oita are presented on a regular basis at the Oita Prefectural Museum of History on a hill called Usa-fudoki-no-oka where visitors can get a good knowledge of the Buddhist culture introduced into Oita.

Izumi-fumoto Samurai Residences

A town for border security developed more than 400 years ago
The shadow of the Edo Period left in a streetscape where many old samurai houses are preserved

The area around Fumotocho in Izumi City, Kagoshima Prefecture is currently a residential area, but it used to be a hilly area at the foot of a mountain castle back in medieval times. More than 400 years ago, a ground-leveling project for this hilly area was implemented by the feudal lords of three generations. After more than 30 years of work, the area was turned into houses and military bases for samurai dispatched to Izumi. Izumi is in an area in the former Satsuma Domain (now Kagoshima Prefecture) and was adjacent to Higo Domain (now Kumamoto Prefecture). Therefore, it was necessary for many samurai to live in Izumi as manpower for border security and emergencies.

So streets and stone walls were formed, to which only small alterations were made even in the modern era. There are many old samurai houses and the gates are still preserved. Therefore, the memory of the Edo Period (1603-1868) remains strongly in the cityscape of the approximately 44 ha area. You can enjoy the atmosphere of Edo just by walking around here, but there are also old samurai houses that you can actually enter, including Takezoe House and Takemiya House, which are partly open to the public, and Saisho

House, which is fully open. It is highly recommended to observe these places and check out the structure of samurai houses in the Edo Period.

Izumi Area

The Izumi Area is a spectacular area to view the crane migrations and visit Bansho Park (Akune City). a former illegal trade security station.

The Izumi Area is located on the northwestern edge of Kagoshima Prefecture and faces the Sea of Yatsushiro. It is famous for the Izumi-fumoto samurai residences dating back to the Edo Period(17th to 19th century) and for being a popular rest site for migratory cranes.

In the early 17th century, stone walls were built around the samural retainer's residences in Izumi-fumoto as protective barricades against invaders from neighboring provinces. Some of these residences still remain today and have been designated as a "Important Preservation District for Group of Historic Buildings" in Japan.

Every autumn, cranes migrate from Siberia and stay until spring. Visitors may observe the cranes fromm the Crane Observation Center. There are multiple exhibits related to cranes on display at Crane Park Izumi, which also has a crane museum and the "Dome Theater" (diameter of 15m) where visitors may experience the virtual flight of a crane

Museum

Ohara Museum of Art

The Ohara Museum of Art was built in 1930 and expanded its original collection of Western paintings and sculptures after the war. It displays works by impressionist painters and other notable 20th-century artists, as well as El Grecos works from the 17th century. "Annunciation" of El Greco and "Woman by Spring" of Pierre-Auguste Renoir are also included in its display. In addition to its Main Gallery, it also has the Annex, Craft Art Gallery, Asiatic Art Gallery and a new exhibition hall. Its collection includes 650 Western-style paintings, 30 sculptures and 370 ceramics from around the world, as well as 320 prints of Shiko Munakata. The Museum also boasts 200 antiques from China and over 1,000 from Egypt and Persia (Iran).'

Information

Address: 1-1-15 chuo, Kurashiki-shi, Okayama

Phone: 086-422-0005

Admission Fee: 1,300 yen

Closed: Monday (except national holidays, Aug., and Oct.)

Dec. 28-31

Notes: [Walk]JR Kurashiki Station/On foot/15 min.

Bizen Pottery Traditional and Contemporary Art Museum

Thrilling techniques and the heart of Bizen Pottery that represents ceramic art of Japan

Bizen Pottery Traditional and Contemporary Art Museum was established with the aim of further developing Bizen pottery that has 1,000 years of history and tradition while at the same time advancing the local culture. Bizen pottery is famous as ash-glaze pottery. Its distinctive feeling of clay has grabbed the heart of many Japanese. The museum exhibits the history and current state of Bizen pottery including the process of creation, changes of kiln and articles from Sueki of the Tumulus Period (250-592) that has developed into Bizen ware to works of unique contemporary ceramics artists.

Must-sees among them are old Bizen Umi-agari (Ship-wreck pots) that were retrieved from the seabed of the Seto Inland Sea, and colored Bizen without artificial coloring that enjoy high popularity as exceptional Bizen. Colored Bizen are very precious articles produced by Okayama clan to present to the Edo Shogunate and other clans during the Edo Period.

Information

Address: 1659-6 Inbe, Bizen-shi, Okayama

Phone: 0869-64-1400

Hours: 9:30-17:00 (admission until 16:30)

Admission Fee: fees: 700 yen (adults); 400 yen (high-school and university students); free admission for junior-high school students and younger

Closed: Monday every week (The next day when Monday falls on a national holiday) and from December 29th to January 3rd

Sea Turtle Museum "Caretta"

Experience the mysterious ecology of sea turtles at a museum built on a coast which is famous as a sea turtle egg laying site

Sea Turtle Museum "Caretta" is one of the few museums in the world devoted to sea turtles. "Caretta" comes from the scientific name for the Loggerhead Sea Turtle, which is designated as a Special Natural Monument. You can learn about the approximately 200 million years of turtle evolution and their mysterious ecology. The first floor exhibits preserved specimens of the world's sea turtles, the process of turtles' evolution, etc. You can also see active turtles ranging from newborn babies to the world's oldest turtle born in 1950. On the second floor, you can see emotional egg laying scenes in a 120 inch high vision theater.

Outdoors, there is a pool where sea turtles over 1 m long are raised, and an artificial hatchery, where they work on artificial hatching of baby turtles. There is also the "Tadayo Sea Turtle Building" with fun facilities like a baby sea turtle water tank and other tanks where from below you can see sea turtles swimming. At sea turtle feeding times, visitors can feed and hug the turtles, so it is very popular among visitors. And the sea turtle shaped phone box in front of the museum is very impressive, making it a popular spot for photos to remember the trip.

Information

Address: 370-4 Hiwasaura, Minami-cho, Kaifu-gun, Tokushima

Phone: 0884-77-1110

Admission Fee: Adults 600 yen, junior high and high school students 500 yen, elementary school students 300 yen, younger children free

Closed: Mondays (closed next day if that Monday is a holiday), Closed for New Year holidays (December 29 to December 31)

Oita Prefectural Art Museum (OPAM)

The brand new Oita Prefectural Art Museum opened in April 2015. Its architecture is designed by a world famous architect Shigeru Ban, who received much attention for the design of the French gallery Centre Pompidou Metz. The collection of OPAM focuses on works by artists who have a close association with Oita Prefecture. This includes modern landscape Nanga style paintings by Chikuden Tanomura, as well as works of the modern Japanese-style painters Heihachiro Fukuda and Tatsuo Takayama.

Information:

Address: 2-1 Kotobuki-machi, Oita-shi, Oita

Hours: 10:00-19:00(admission until 18:30)

Friday and Saturday 10:00-20:00 (admission until 19:30)

Admission Fee: None

Collection Exhibition

Adults 300 yen

College students and high school students 200 yen

Special Exhibition

Depends on each exhibition

Closed: Mondays (if the Monday is a national holiday, the following weekday), New Years holidays, maintenance period.

Otsuka Museum of Art

Otsuka Museum of Art was built by Otsuka Pharmaceutical Group to commemorate the companys 75th anniversary. With a total floor area of 29,412 square meters, the museum has the largest exhibition space in Japan. Its collection of more than 1,000 reproductions of Western masterpieces on ceramic boards comprises the works from 190 museums in 25 countries and was selected by 6 acclaimed art historians. Using a special manufacturing technique, images of the masterpieces were replicated on the ceramic boards in original size.

One of the highlights of the museum would be the complete reproduction of Michelangelo's ceiling and The Last Judgment in Sistine Chapel in full scale. Along with this, visitors can appreciate the beauty of Claude Monet's Water Lilies, the serenity of the works of Giotto of Scrovegni Chapel in Padua, Italy, powerful dominance of Picasso's "Guernica" which never leaves the Museo Nacional Centro de Arte Reina Sofia,Madrid and Leonardo da Vinci's The Last Supper before and after latest restoration would be viewed in full scale as well. The museum is located in the national park of Naruto over looking the Inland Sea. It is filled with natural beauty of the landscape and also known as the famous bird sanctuary.

Information

Address: The National Park, Naruto-cho, Naruto-shi, Tokushima

Admission Fee: 3240 yen (Adults)/2160yen (University students)/540yen (Elementary, Junior High School students)

Closed: Mondays (if the Monday is a national holiday, the following weekday)

Notes: [Bus]JR Tokushima Stn./Bus/55-min. ride/Otsuka Kokusai Bijutukan(Otsuka International Museum of Art) Stop

Okayama-shiritsu Orient Bijutsukan

Okayama-shiritsu Orient Bijutsukan (The Okayama Municipal Orient Museum) was built to house a collection of "art of the Orient" donated in 1947. The museum is distinguished by the scientifically systematized layout of this diverse collection, which includes information from various fields indispensable to the understanding of aspects of non-Western culture. The permanent exhibition, entitled The History and Culture of the Orient, presents in chronological order a variety of artworks unearthed in the Middle East, the cradle of civilization. These are divided into four sections: From Hunter-Gathers to Farmer-Herders, City Formation and the Development of the Ancient Empires, Hellenism and Persian Culture, and The Islamic Age.

Information

Address: 9-31 Tenjin-cho, Kita-ku, Okayama-shi, Okayama

Admission Fee: 300 yen (permanent exhibition)

Closed: Mondays (if the Monday is a national holiday, the following weekday), New Years holidays, maintenance period

Okayama Kenritsu Bijutsukan (Art Museum)

Okayama Kenritsu Bijutsukan (The Okayama Prefectural Museum of Art) is located in the city center of Okayama, near Okayama Castle and Korakuen, one of the three most famous gardens in Japan. It houses mostly works by artists closely connected to Okayama Prefecture. The collection covers an extensive period from the Middle Ages to modern times, with pieces by many different artists. On display here is the work entitled Matsuri wa Owatta (The Festival is Over) by Yasuo Kuniyoshi, an example of Western-style painting by a Japanese artist.

Born in 1889 in Okayama, Kuniyoshi traveled to America and worked actively there, eventually becoming famous worldwide for his original style. The museum also holds Japanese-style paintings, including Sesshus Sansui-zu (Painting of a Landscape), designated an Important Cultural Property by the Japanese government, which is said to have been painted in the latter half of the 15th century, and Hotei-zu, a painting of a potbellied god who is one of the Seven Deities of Fortune, by Miyamoto Musashi. Miyamoto was also known as a master swordsman, and the work is thought to have been painted in the first half of the 17th century.'

Information

Address: 8-48 Tenjin-cho, Kita-ku, Okayama-shi, Okayama

Admission Fee: 300 yen (permanent exhibition)

Closed: Mondays (if the Monday is a national holiday, the following weekday), New Years holidays, maintenance period'

Hyuga City History and Folk Museum

From the Edo period (1603-1868) to the Meiji period (1868-1912), the port town of Mimitsu flourished as a hub for trade with the Kansai region. The cityscape of its heyday remains even today, including buildings, walls, and stone pavements, and it has been designated as a national important preservation district for groups of historic buildings.

Located at the center of this preservation district, the Hyuga City History and Folk Museum is housed in a building restored in 1982, which was built at the end of the Edo period for a shipping agent business, and now displays various items in its collection. It replicates various aspects of merchant houses of the time, including the courtyard with a small man-made hill and ornamental rocks, as well as a hanare, or separate villa. Incorporating many aspects of the architectural style typical of the machiya townhouses of Kyoto and Osaka, such as hako-kaidan step chests, mushikomado finely-latticed top-floor windows, and kyogoshi latticed windows, this building is well worth a look.

In addition, the exhibits inside the building include ledgers, abacuses, writing desks, and various other tools of commerce, as well as historic and folk artifacts, and archaeological materials dating from the Jomon period to the Kofun period. The second floor affords a view out over the sea at Mimitsu. In the preservation district, you can also visit the Mimitsu-ken, which occupies a machiya-style townhouse, and the Mimitsu Machinami Center, in what was once a shop dealing in kimono fabric. We heartily recommend that you take a leisurely stroll through this atmospheric townscape that will make you think you've stepped back in time.

Information

Address: 3244 Mimitsu-cho, Hyuga City, Miyazaki

Phone: 0982-58-0443

Hours: 9:00 - 16:30

Admission Fee: Adults 210 yen, High school students and below 100 yen

Closed: Mondays (if it's national holiday, day after monday), New Year holidays

Hokkaido Museum of Modern Art

Hokkaido Museum of Modern Art is located on the west side of Sapporo Odori Park, in the city of Sapporo. The white tile building was designed to match the areas snowy winter landscape. The collection at this museum is founded on three fundamental principles: first, to collect works of artists from Hokkaido; second, to collect works of the Ecole de Paris, including those of Pascin, Utrillo, Dongen, Kisling, Soutine and Laurencin; and third, to collect glassware representing periods from Art Nouveau through contemporary. In addition to exhibiting works of art, this museum also attaches important to art education. Each day volunteer guides accompany visitors as they walk through the museum, informing them about the works of art on display. (These tours are only available in Japanese.)

The museum is closed from September 2011 to January 2012 for reconstruction.

Information

Address: 17 chome, Kita-Ichijo-nishi, Chuo-ku, Sapporo-shi, Hokkaido

Admission Fee: 450 yen (permanent exhibition)

Closed: Mondays (if the Monday is a national holiday, the following weekday), New Years holidays, maintenance period'

Notes: [Rail]JR Sapporo Stn./Sapporo Shiei Subway Nanboku Line/2-min. ride/O-dori Stn./Sapporo Shiei Subway Tozai Line/4-min. ride/Nishi 18-chome Stn./5-min. walk

Migishi Kotaro Museum of Art

Migishi Kotaro Museum of Art is located in the city of Sapporo, Hokkaido. The gallery collection consists mainly of artworks by Migishi Kotaro, a self-taught painter born in Sapporo in 1903. He is regarded as a pioneer of avant-garde art. He died at the young age of 31, but during the short period of 12 years in which he was painting, his style went through many changes, and later in life he produced a number of surrealist works. The collection was donated by Migishi's family after his death, and the gallery opened on 1 July 1983, exactly fifty years after he passed away. White walls, a glassy lobby, and a light gray interior create a space befitting an artist with a love for the modern.'

Information
Address: Nishi 15-chome, Kita 2-jo, Chuo-ku, Sapporo-shi, Hokkaido
Admission Fee: 500 yen (permanent exhibition)
Closed: Mondays, New Years holidays, maintenance period'
Notes: [Rail]JR Sapporo Stn./Sapporo Shiei Subway Nanboku Line/2-min. ride/Odori Stn./Sapporo Shiei Subway Tozai Line/4-min. ride/Nishi 18-chome Stn./5-min. walk

Tokyo National Museum

Tokyo National Museum (TNM) began in 1872 with an exposition held at the Yushima Seido Confucian shrine in Tokyo. It has the longest history among all museums in Japan. TNM collects, preserves, restores and displays art, archaeological objects and other cultural properties from Japan and across Asia. The museum also conducts research into these properties and promotes understanding of them through educational activities.

The TNM collection comprises around 114,000 items, including 87 National Treasures and 633 Important Cultural Properties (as of March 2014). It is the best collection of cultural properties in Japan in terms of both quality and number. The Regular Exhibition galleries exhibit about 4,000 of these works at any given time.

Information

Address: 13-9 Ueno-koen, Taito-ku, Tokyo

Hours: 9:30 a.m. - 5:00 p.m. (Open until 8:00 p.m. on Fridays and Saturdays) (Last admission 30 minutes before closing)

Admission Fee: 620 yen (regular fee), Special exhibitions require a separate admission fee

Closed: Mondays (if the Monday is a national holiday, the following day), Year-end holidays (Dec. 24, 2014 - Jan. 1, 2015)

Notes: [Rail]JR Tokyo Stn. / Yamanote Line / 8-min. ride / Ueno Stn. / 10-min. walk

Kyoto National Museum

The Kyoto National Museum, located in Japan's ancient capital of Kyoto, collects and preserves venerable works of art and archaeological artifacts from Japan as well as other Asian countries. The primary focus of the museum collections is the millennium during which Kyoto was the capital of Japan, from 794 to 1868. The original museum building, known today as the Meiji Kotokan, is a red brick hall in the French Renaissance style, which opened in 1897. It was designed by the architect Katayama Tokuma, who contributed greatly to the introduction of Western architecture to Japan.

The Meiji Kotokan, together with the red brick Main Gate and part of the surrounding wall, was designated an Important Cultural Property in 1969 by the Japanese government. Today it is used for special exhibitions in the spring and autumn and sometimes other parts of the year. In September 2014, the museum opened an elegant, contemporary new wing called the Heisei Chishinkan, designed by architect Taniguchi Yoshio. The new wing is used for regularly changing thematic exhibitions of the collections, which include both museum-owned works and works entrusted to the museum on long-term loan from temples and shrines in Kyoto, the Kansai region, and other parts of the country.

Information

Address: 527 Chaya-cho, Higashiyama-ku, Kyoto-shi, Kyoto

Hours: 9:30 a.m. - 5:00 p.m. (Open until 8:00 p.m. on Fridays and Saturdays) (Last admission 30 minutes before closing)

Hours may change according to the exhibition

Admission Fee: 520 yen (regular fee), Special exhibitions require a separate admission fee

Closed: Mondays (if the Monday is a national holiday, the following day), New Years holidays

Notes: [Bus]JR Kyoto Stn. / Bus / 5-min. ride / Hakubutsukan Sanjusangendo-mae Stop / 3-min. walk

Calendar of Events

January

New Year's Da: is the most important national holiday in Japan. Because this is a time when Japanese are with their families and because virtually all businesses, restaurants, museums, and shops close down, it's not a particularly rewarding time of the year for foreign visitors. Best bets are shrines and temples, where Japanese come in their best kimono or dress to pray for good health and happiness in the coming year. January 1.

Tamaseseri (Ball-Catching Festival): Hakozakigu Shrine, Fukuoka. The main attraction here is a struggle between two groups of men, dressed only in loincloths, who try to capture a sacred wooden ball.

The winning team is supposed to have good luck the entire year. January 3.

Dezomeshiki (New Year's Parade of Firemen): Tokyo Big Sight, Odaiba, Tokyo. Agile firemen dressed in Edo-Era costumes prove their worth with acrobatic stunts atop tall bamboo ladders in this parade. January 6.

Usokae (Bullfinch Exchange Festival): Dazaifu Tenmangu Shrine, outside Fukuoka. The object here is to pass wooden bullfinches from person to person, hopefully ending up with the golden bullfinch, thought to bring good luck. A giant fire is lit in the evening to drive away evil spirits. January 7.

Coming-of-Age Day: a national holiday. This day honors young people who have reached the age of 20, when they can vote, drink alcohol, and assume other responsibilities. On this day, they visit shrines throughout the country to pray for their future, with many women dressed in kimono. In Tokyo, the most popular shrine is Meiji Shrine near Harajuku Station. Second Monday in January.

Toka Ebisu Festival: Imamiya Ebisu Shrine, Osaka. Ebisu is considered the patron saint of business and good fortune, so this is the time when businesspeople pray for a successful year. The highlight of the festival is a parade of women dressed in colorful kimono and carried through the streets in palanquins (covered litters). Stalls sell good-luck charms. January 9 to January 11.

Ame-Ichi (Candy Fair): Matsumoto. Formerly a salt fair, this lively festival has featured traditional candy for the past century. Second weekend in January.

Toh-shiya: Kyoto. This traditional Japanese archery contest is held in the back corridor of Japan's longest wooden structure, Sanjusangendo Hall. Sunday closest to January 15.

Yamayaki (Grass Fire Ceremony): Nara. As evening approaches, Wakakusayama Hill is set ablaze and fireworks are displayed. The celebration marks a time more than 1,000 years ago when a dispute over the boundary of two major temples in Nara was settled peacefully. Fourth Sunday in January.

Sounkyo Ice Festival: Sounkyo Onsen. Ice sculptures, ice slides, frozen waterfalls lit in various colors, and evening fireworks are the highlights of this small-town festival. Mid-January to Mid-March.

February

Oyster Festival: Matsushima. Matsushima is famous for its oysters, and this is the time they're considered to be at their best. Oysters are given out free at booths set up at the seaside park along the bay. First Sunday in February.

Setsubun (Bean-Throwing Festival): at leading temples throughout Japan. According to the lunar calendar, this is the last day of winter; people throng to temples to participate in the traditional ceremony of throwing beans to drive away imaginary devils, yelling, "Evil go out, good luck come in." February 3 or 4.

Lantern Festival: Kasuga Shrine, Nara. A beautiful sight in which more than 3,000 stone and bronze lanterns are lit from 6:30 to 9pm. February 3 and August 14 and 15.

Snow Festival: Odori Park, and Susukino, in Sapporo. This famous 7-day Sapporo festival features huge, elaborate statues and figurines carved in snow and ice. Competitors come from around the world. Second week in February.

Saidaiji Eyo: Saidaiji Kannon-in Temple, Okayama. Thousands of loincloth-clad men grapple for sacred wooden sticks tossed by priests. Third Saturday of February at midnight.

March

Omizutori (Water-Drawing Festival): Todaiji Temple, Nara. This festival includes a solemn evening rite in which young ascetics brandish large burning torches and draw circles of fire. The biggest ceremony takes place on the night of March 12; on the next day, the ceremony of drawing water is held to the accompaniment of ancient Japanese music. March 1 to March 14.

Hinamatsuri (Doll Festival): observed throughout Japan. It's held in honor of young girls to wish them a future of happiness. In homes where there are girls, dolls dressed in ancient costumes representing the emperor, empress, and dignitaries are set up on a tier of shelves along with miniature household articles. Many hotels also display dolls in their lobbies. March 3.

Tokyo International Anime Fair: Tokyo Big Sight, Odaiba (www.tokyoanime.jp). One of the world's largest Japanese animation events draws more than 100 production companies, TV and film agencies, toy and game software companies, publishers, and other *anime*-related companies. Usually last weekend in March.

April

Kanamara Matsuri: Kanayama Shrine, Kawasaki (just outside Tokyo). This festival extols the joys of sex and fertility (and more recently, raises awareness about AIDS), featuring a parade of giant phalluses, some carried by transvestites. You'll definitely get some unusual photographs here. First Sunday in April.

Buddha's Birthday: (also called Hana Matsuri, or Floral Festival), observed nationwide. Ceremonies are held at all Buddhist temples. April 8.

Kamakura Matsuri: Tsurugaoka Hachimangu Shrine, Kamakura. This festival honors heroes from the past, including Minamoto Yoritomo, who made Kamakura his shogunate capital back in 1192. Highlights include horseback archery (truly spectacular to watch), a parade of portable shrines, and sacred dances. Second to third Sunday of April.

Takayama Spring Festival: Takayama. Supposedly dating from the 15th century, this festival is one of Japan's grandest with a dozen huge, gorgeous floats that are wheeled through the village streets. April 14 and 15.

Gumonji-do (Firewalking Ceremonies): Miyajima. Walking on live coals is meant to show devotion and to pray for purification and protection from illness and disaster. Daishoin Temple. April 15 and November 15.

Yayoi Matsuri: Futarasan Shrine, Nikko. Yayoi Matsuri features a parade of floats embellished with artificial cherry blossoms and paper lanterns. April 16 and 17.

Golden Wee: is a major holiday period throughout Japan, when many Japanese offices and businesses close down and families go on vacation. It's a crowded time to travel; reservations are a must. April 29 to May 5.

May

Hakata Dontaku Port Festival: Fukuoka. Citizens, dressed as deities, parade through the streets clapping wooden rice paddles. May 3 and 4.

Children's Day: is a national holiday honoring all children, especially boys. The most common sight throughout Japan is colorful streamers of carp which symbolize perseverance and strength flying from poles. May 5.

Takigi Noh Performances: Kofukuji Temple, Nara. These *noh* plays are presented outdoors after dark under the blaze of torches. May 11 and 12.

Kanda Festival: Kanda Myojin Shrine, Tokyo. This festival, which commemorates Tokugawa Ieyasu's famous victory at Sekigahara in 1600, began during the Feudal Period as the only time townspeople could enter the shogun's castle and parade before him. Today this major Tokyo festival features a parade of dozens of portable shrines carried through the district, plus geisha dances and a tea ceremony.

Held in odd-numbered years (with a smaller festival held in even years) on the Saturday and Sunday closest to May 15.

Aoi Matsuri (Hollyhock Festival): Shimogamo and Kamigamo Shrines, Kyoto. This is one of Kyoto's biggest events, a colorful parade with 500 participants wearing ancient costumes to commemorate the days when the imperial procession visited the city's shrines. May 15.

Kobe Matsuri: Kobe. This relatively new festival celebrates Kobe's international past with fireworks at Kobe Port, street markets, and a parade on Flower Road with participants wearing native costumes. Mid-May.

Shunki Reitaisai (Grand Spring Festival): Nikko. Commemorating the day in 1617 when Tokugawa Ieyasu's remains were brought to his mausoleum in Nikko, this festival re-creates that drama with more than 1,000 armor-clad people escorting three palanquins through the streets. May 17 and 18.

Sanja Matsuri: Asakusa Shrine, Tokyo. Tokyo's most celebrated festival features about 100 portable shrines carried through the district on the shoulders of men and women in traditional garb. Third Sunday and preceding Friday and Saturday of May.

Mifune Matsuri: Arashiyama, on the Oigawa River outside Kyoto, is when the days of the Heian Period (during which the imperial family used to take pleasure rides on the river) are reenacted by some 20 boats and people in costume. Third Sunday in May.

June

Takigi Noh Performances: Kyoto. Evening performances of *noh* are presented on an open-air stage at the Heian Shrine. June 1 and 2.

Hyakumangoku Matsuri (One Million Goku Festival): Kanazawa. Celebrating Kanazawa's production of one million *goku* of rice (1 goku is about 150kg/330 lb.), this extravaganza features folk songs and traditional dancing in the streets, illuminated paper lanterns floating downriver, public tea ceremonies, geisha performances, and the highlight a parade that winds through the city in reenactment of Lord Maeda Toshiie's triumphant arrival in Kanazawa on June 14, 1583, with lion dances, ladder-top acrobatics by firemen, and a torch-lit outdoor *noh* performance. June 8 to June 14.

Sanno Festival: Hie Shrine, Tokyo. This Edo Period festival, one of Tokyo's largest, features the usual portable shrines, transported through the busy streets of the Akasaka District. June 10 to June 16.

Otaue Rice-Planting Festival: Sumiyoshi Taisha Shrine, Osaka. In hopes of a successful harvest, young girls in traditional farmers' costumes transplant rice seedlings in the shrine's rice paddy to the sound of traditional music and songs. June 14.

Ukai (Cormorant Fishing): Nagara River near Gifu and Kiso River in Inuyama (near Nagoya). Visitors board small wooden boats after dark to watch cormorants dive into the water to catch *ayu,* a kind of trout. Generally end of May to October.

July

Tanabata Matsuri (Star Festival): celebrated throughout Japan. According to myth, the two stars Vega and Altair, representing a weaver and a shepherd, are allowed to meet once a year on this day. If the skies are cloudy, however, the celestial pair cannot meet and must wait another year. Celebrations differ from town to town, but in addition to parades and food/souvenir stalls, look for bamboo branches with colorful strips of paper bearing children's wishes. July 7.

Hozuki Ichi (Ground-Cherry Pod Fair): Tokyo. This colorful affair at Sensoji Temple in Asakusa features hundreds of stalls selling ground-cherry pods and colorful wind bells. July 9 and 10.

Yamakasa: Fukuoka. Just before the crack of dawn, seven teams dressed in loincloths and *happi* coats (short, colorful, kimono-like jackets) race through town, bearing 1-ton floats on their shoulders. In addition, elaborately decorated, 9m-tall (30-ft.) floats designed by Hakata doll masters are on display throughout town. July 15.

Gion Matsuri: Kyoto. One of the most famous festivals in Japan, this dates back to the 9th century, when the head priest at Yasaka Shrine organized a procession to ask the gods' assistance in a plague raging in the city. Although celebrations continue throughout the month, the highlight is on the 17th, when more than 30 spectacular wheeled floats wind their way through the city streets to the accompaniment of music and dances. Many visitors plan their trip to Japan around this event. July 16 and 17.

Obon Festival: nationwide. This festival commemorates the dead who, according to Buddhist belief, revisit the world during this period. Many Japanese return to their hometowns for religious rites, especially if a family member has died recently. As one Japanese whose grandmother had died a few months before told me, "I have to go back to my hometown it's my grandmother's first Obon." Mid-July or mid-August, depending on the region.

Tenjin Matsuri: Temmangu Shrine, Osaka. One of Japan's biggest festivals, this dates from the 10th century when the people of Osaka visited Temmangu Shrine to pray for protection against diseases prevalent during the long, hot summer. They would take pieces of paper cut in the form of human beings and, while the Shinto priest said prayers, would rub the paper over themselves in ritual cleansing. Afterward, the pieces of paper were taken by boat to the mouth of the river and disposed of. Today, events are reenacted with a procession of more than 100 sacred boats making their way downriver, followed by a fireworks display. There's also a parade of some 3,000 people in traditional costume. July 24 and 25.

Kangensai Music Festival: Itsukushima Shrine, Miyajima. There are classical court music and *Bugaku* dancing, and three barges carry portable shrines, priests, and musicians across the bay along with a flotilla of other boats. Because this festival takes place according to the lunar calendar, the actual date changes each year. Late July or early August.

Hanabi Taikai (Fireworks Display): Tokyo. This is Tokyo's largest summer celebration, and everyone sits on blankets along the banks of the Sumida River near Asakusa to see the show. It's great fun! Last Saturday of July.

Fuji Rock Festival: Naeba Ski Resort, Niigata. Japan's biggest outdoor rock festival, with an impressive lineup of international acts in a beautiful mountain setting. Last weekend in July.

August

Oshiro Matsuri: Himeji. This celebration is famous for its *noh* dramas lit by bonfire and performed on a special stage on the Himeji Castle grounds, as well as a procession from the castle to the city center with participants dressed as feudal lords and ladies in traditional costume. First Friday and Saturday of August.

Peace Ceremony: Peace Memorial Park, Hiroshima. This ceremony is held annually in memory of those who died in the atomic bomb blast of August 6, 1945. In the evening, thousands of lit lanterns are set adrift on the Ota River in a plea for world peace. A similar ceremony is held on August 9 in Nagasaki. August 6.

Tanabata Matsuri: Sendai. Sendai holds its Star Festival 1 month later than the rest of Japan. It's the country's largest, and the entire town is decorated with colored paper streamers. August 6 to August 8.

Matsuyama Festival: Matsuyama. Jubilant festivities include dances, fireworks, a parade, and a night fair. August 11 to August 13.

Takamatsu Festival: Takamatsu. About 6,000 people participate in a dance procession that threads its way along Chuo Dori Avenue; anyone can join in. Food stalls are set up in Chuo Park, and there's also a fireworks display. August 12 to August 14.

Toronagashi and Fireworks Display: Matsushima. A fireworks display is followed by the setting adrift on the bay of about 5,000 small boats with lanterns, which are meant to console the souls of the dead; another 3,000 lanterns are lit on islets in the bay. Evening of August 15.

Yamaga Lantern Festival: Kumamoto. Women dressed in *yukata* dance through town with illuminated paper lanterns on their heads, and there's also a fireworks display. August 15 and 16.

Daimonji Bonfire: Mount Nyoigadake, Kyoto. A huge bonfire in the shape of the Chinese character *dai,* which means "large," and other motifs are lit near mountain peaks; it's the highlight of the Obon Festival. August 16.

Eisa Festival, Okinawa Island. Dance teams compete in lively folk performances to the accompaniment of drums, three-stringed *sanshin,* and other instruments. Late August.

September

Yabusame: Tsurugaoka Hachimangu Shrine, Kamakura. Archery performed on horseback recalls the days of the samurai. September 16.

October

Okunchi Festival: Suwa Shrine, Nagasaki. This 370-year-old festival, one of Kyushu's best, illustrates the influence of Nagasaki's Chinese population through the centuries. Highlights include a parade of floats and dragon dances. October 7 to October 9.

Marimo Matsuri: Lake Akan, Hokkaido. This festival is put on by the native Ainu population to celebrate *marimo* (a spherical weed found in Lake Akan) and includes a pine torch parade and fireworks. Early October.

Takayama Matsuri (Autumn Festival): Takayama. As in the festival held here in April, huge floats are paraded through the streets. October 9 and 10.

Nagoya Festival, Nagoya: Nagoya's biggest event commemorates three of its heroes Tokugawa Ieyasu, Toyotomi Hideyoshi, and Oda Nobunaga in a parade that goes from City Hall to Sakae and includes nine floats with mechanical puppets, marching bands, and a traditional orchestra. Second weekend in October.

Naha Tug of War: Naha, Okinawa. Anyone can join in this tug of war with the world's largest rope (186m/619 ft.), once held to welcome Chinese ambassadors. Second Sunday in October.

Nada no Kenka Matsuri (Nada Fighting Festival): Matsubara Hachiman Shrine, Himeji. Men shouldering portable shrines jostle each other as they attempt to show their skill in balancing their heavy burdens. October 14 and 15.

Doburoku Matsuri: Ogimachi, Shirakawago. This village festival honors unrefined sake, said to represent the spirit of God, with a parade, an evening lion dance, and plenty of eating and drinking. October 14 to October 19.

Nikko Toshogu Shrine Festival: Nikko. A parade of warriors in early-17th-century dress are accompanied by spear-carriers, gun-carriers, flag-bearers, Shinto priests, pages, court musicians, and dancers as they escort a sacred portable shrine. October 17.

Jidai Matsuri (Festival of the Ages): Kyoto. Another of Kyoto's grand festivals, this one began in 1894 to commemorate the founding of the city in 794. It features a procession of more than 2,000 people dressed in ancient costumes representing different epochs of Kyoto's 1,200-year history, who march from the Imperial Palace to Heian Shrine. October 22.

November

Ohara Matsuri: Kagoshima. About 15,000 people parade through the town in cotton *yukata,* dancing to the tune of local folk songs. A sort of Japanese Mardi Gras, this event attracts several hundred thousand spectators each year. November 2 and 3.

Daimyo Gyoretsu (Feudal Lord Procession): Yumoto Onsen, Hakone. The old Tokaido Highway that used to link Kyoto and Tokyo comes alive again with a faithful reproduction of a feudal lord's procession in the olden days. November 3.

Shichi-go-san (Children's Shrine-Visiting Day): held throughout Japan. Shichi-go-san literally means "seven-five-three" and refers to children of these ages who are dressed in their kimono best and taken to shrines by their elders to express thanks and pray for their future. November 15.

Tori-no-Ichi (Rake Fair): Otori Shrine, Tokyo. This fair in Asakusa features stalls selling rakes lavishly decorated with paper and cloth, which are thought to bring good luck and fortune. Based on the lunar calendar, the date changes each year. Mid-November.

December

Gishi-sai: Sengakuji Station, Tokyo. This memorial service honors 47 *ronin*(masterless samurai) who avenged their master's death by killing his rival and parading his head; for their act, all were ordered to commit suicide. Forty-seven men dressed as the ronin travel to

Sengakuji Temple (the site of their and their master's burial) with the enemy's head to place on their master's grave. December 14.

Kasuga Wakamiya On-Matsuri: Kasuga Shrine, Nara. This festival features court music with traditional dance and a parade of people dressed as courtiers, retainers, and wrestlers of long ago. December 15 to December 18.

Hagoita-Ichi (Battledore Fair): Sensoji Temple, Tokyo. Popular since Japan's feudal days, this Asakusa festival features decorated paddles of all types and sizes. Most have designs of kabuki actors images made by pasting together padded silk and brocade and make great souvenirs and gifts. December 17 to December 19.

New Year's Eve: At midnight, many temples ring huge bells 108 times to signal the end of the old year and the beginning of the new. Families visit temples and shrines throughout Japan to pray for the coming year. December 31.

The Best among All
My favourite Experiences

Long ago, Japanese ranked the three best of almost every natural wonder and attraction in their country: the three best gardens, the three best scenic spots, the three best waterfalls, even the three best bridges. But choosing the "best" of anything is inherently subjective, and decades even centuries have passed since some of the original "three best" were so designated. Still, lists can be useful for establishing priorities. To help you get the most out of your stay, I've compiled this list of what I consider the best Japan has to offer based on years of traveling through the country. From the weird to the wonderful, the profound to the profane, the obvious to the obscure, these recommendations should fire your imagination and launch you toward discoveries of your own.

Making a Pilgrimage to a Temple or Shrine: From mountaintop shrines to neighborhood temples, Japan's religious structures rank among the nation's most popular attractions. Usually devoted to a particular deity, they're visited for specific reasons: Shopkeepers call on Fushimi-Inari Shrine outside Kyoto, dedicated to the goddess of rice and therefore prosperity, while couples wishing for a happy marriage head to Kyoto's Jishu Shrine, a shrine to the deity of love. Shrines and temples are also the sites for Japan's major festivals.

Taking a Communal Hot-Spring Bath: No other people on earth bathe as enthusiastically, as frequently, and for such duration as Japanese. Their many hot-spring baths thought to cure all sorts of ailments as well as simply make you feel good range from elegant, Zen-like affairs to rustic outdoor baths with views of the countryside. No matter what the setup, you'll soon warm to the ritual of soaping up, rinsing off, and then soaking in near-scalding waters. Hot-spring spas are located almost everywhere in Japan, from Kyushu to Hokkaido.

Participating in a Festival: With Shintoism and Buddhism as its major religions, and temples and shrines virtually everywhere, Japan has multiple festivals every week. These celebrations, which range from huge processions of wheeled floats to those featuring horseback archery and ladder-top acrobatics, can be lots of fun; you may want to plan your trip around one (and book early for a hotel).

Dining on Japanese Food: There's more to Japanese cuisine than sushi, and part of what makes travel here so fascinating is the variety of national and regional dishes. Every prefecture, it seems, has its own style of noodles, its special vegetables, and its delicacies. If money is no object, order *kaiseki,* a complete meal of visual and culinary finesse.

Viewing the Cherry Blossoms: Nothing symbolizes the approach of spring so vividly to Japanese as the appearance of the cherry blossoms and nothing so amazes visitors as the way Japanese gather under the blossoms to celebrate the season with food, drink, and dance.

Riding the Shinkansen Bullet Train: Asia's fastest train whips you across the countryside at more than 290km (180 miles) an hour as you relax, see Japan's rural countryside, and dine on boxed meals filled with local specialties.

Staying in a Ryokan: Japan's legendary service reigns supreme in a top-class *ryokan,* a traditional Japanese inn. You'll bathe in a Japanese tub or hot-spring bath, feast your eyes on lovely views past *shoji* screens, dine like a king in your *tatami* room, and sleep on a futon.

Shopping in a Department Store: Japan's department stores are among the best in the world, offering everything from food to designer clothing to electronics to kimono and traditional crafts. Service also is among the best in the world: If you arrive when the store opens, staff will be lined up at the front door to bow as you enter.

Visiting a Local Market: Tsukiji Fish Market, in Tokyo, is Japan's largest, but there are local seafood and produce markets virtually everywhere. Those in Kyoto, Kanazawa, Takayama, Hakodate, and Okinawa are among my favorites.

Attending a Kabuki Play: Based on universal themes and designed to appeal to the masses, *kabuki* plays are extravaganzas of theatrical displays, costumes, and scenes but mostly they're just plain fun.

Strolling Through Tokyo's Nightlife District: Every major city in Japan has its own nightlife district, but probably none is more famous, more wicked, or more varied than Tokyo's Shinjuku, which offers everything from hole-in-the-wall bars to strip joints, dance clubs, and gay clubs.

Seeing Mount Fuji: It may not seem like much of an accomplishment to see Japan's most famous and tallest mountain, visible from about 150km (100 miles) away. But, the truth is, it's hardly ever visible, except during the winter months and rare occasions when the air is clear. Catching your first glimpse of the giant peak is truly breathtaking and something you'll never forget, whether you see it from aboard the Shinkansen, a Tokyo skyscraper, or a nearby national park. If you want to climb it (possible only in July-Aug), be prepared for a group experience 400,000 people climb Mount Fuji every summer.

Spending a Few Days in Kyoto: If you see only one city in Japan, Kyoto should be it. Japan's capital from 794 to 1868, Kyoto is one of Japan's finest ancient cities, boasting some of the country's best temples, Japanese-style inns, traditional restaurants, shops, and gardens.

The Best Museums

Edo-Tokyo Museum (Tokyo): Housed in a high-tech modern building, this ambitious museum chronicles the fascinating and somewhat tumultuous history of Tokyo (known as Edo during the Feudal Era) with models, replicas, artifacts, and dioramas. Volunteers stand ready to give free guided tours in English.

Tokyo National Museum (Tokyo): Even professed museumphobes should make a point of visiting the National Museum, the largest repository of Japanese arts in the world. Lacquerware, china, kimono, samurai armor, swords, woodblock prints, religious art, and more are on display, making this the best place in Japan to view Japanese antiques and decorative objects. If you visit only one museum in Japan, this should be it.

Hakone Open-Air Museum (Chokoku-no-Mori, Hakone): Beautifully landscaped grounds and spectacular scenery showcase approximately 400 20th-century sculptures, from Giacomo and Rodin to Henry Moore. Here, too, is the Picasso Pavilion, housing 200 of the artist's works.

Japan Ukiyo-e Museum (Matsumoto): One of the best woodblock-print museums in Japan, this museum displays the largest collection of prints in the world on a rotating basis. A must-see in Matsumoto.

Hida Folk Village (Takayama): Picturesquely situated around a pond with flowers, more than 30 shingled and thatched farmhouses many transported from the surrounding Japan Alps are filled with farm implements and objects of daily life, providing fascinating insight into the life and times of the extended families that once inhabited them.

Museum Meiji Mura (Nagoya): This open-air architectural museum is an absolute treasure, with more than 60 original buildings and structures dating from the Meiji Period situated on 100 hectares (250 acres) that are beautifully landscaped on the shore of a lake. Western-style homes, churches, a kabuki theater, a bathhouse, a prison, a brewery, and much more are open for viewing and filled with furniture and household items. Mail a postcard from an authentic post office, buy candy from an old candy store, and drink tea in the lobby of the original Imperial Hotel, which was designed by Frank Lloyd Wright.

Ishikawa Prefectural Museum for Traditional Products and Crafts(Kanazawa): Kanazawa is famous for its handcrafted items, including gold leaf, umbrellas, stringed instruments, Buddhist altars, pottery, and more. English-language explanations and an audio guide explain how they're made.

Disaster Reduction Museum (Kobe): You can't tell by its name, but this excellent museum is devoted to Kobe's 1995 earthquake, with films, dioramas, and exhibits detailing the city's destruction and rebirth.

Ohara Museum of Art (Kurashiki): Founded in 1930, this museum just keeps getting bigger and better, with works by both Western and

Japanese greats spread throughout several buildings. Its location in the picturesque Kurashiki historic district is a bonus.

Adachi Museum (Matsue): This museum near Matsue combines two of my passions art and gardens making it a winner. Japanese modern art is the focus indoors, while the perfectly landscaped garden one of Japan's best comes into view through framed windows, making it part of the art in a very surreal way.

Peace Memorial Museum (Hiroshima): Japan's most thought-provoking museum contains exhibits examining Hiroshima's militaristic past, the events leading up to the explosion of the world's first atomic bomb, the city's terrible destruction, and its active antinuclear movement.

Benesse Art Site Naoshima (Takamatsu): This is not a single museum, but rather an island in the Seto Inland Sea that's devoted to cutting-edge art, with two museums (both designed by Tadao Ando) and interactive art installations in traditional Japanese buildings. There's no other place in Japan quite like this

The Best National Parks

Nikko National Park: This 80,000-hectare (200,000-acre) national park centers on the sumptuous Toshogu Shrine with its mausoleum for Tokugawa Ieyasu, majestic cedars, and lakeside resorts.

Fuji-Hakone-Izu National Park: Boasting magnificent Mount Fuji at its core, this popular weekend getaway beckons vacationing Tokyoites with its many hot-spring spas, stunning close-up views of Mount Fuji, sparkling lakes, historic attractions relating to the famous Feudal-Era Tokaido Highway, and coastal areas of Izu Peninsula. One of the best ways to see Hakone is via a circular route that involves travel on a two-car mountain streetcar, a cable car, a ropeway, and a boat; the delightful journey offers wonderful scenery and interesting sights along the way.

Japan Alps (Chubu Sangaku) National Park: Encompassing Honshu's most impressive mountain ranges and the site of the 1998 Winter Olympics, this national park offers skiing and hiking as well as unique villages worth a visit in their own right.

Ise-Shima National Park: Boasting a rugged seascape of capes, inlets, and islets, this park is the birthplace of cultivated pearls. It's famous for its bays dotted with pearl-cultivating oyster rafts, its female divers, a pearl museum, plus a top-notch aquarium and the Ise Grand Shrines,

Japan's most venerable shrines. Two theme parks are also located here.

Seto-Naikai (Inland Sea) National Park: Covering 650 sq. km (251 sq. miles) of water, islands, islets, and coastline, this sea park stretches from Kobe in the east to Beppu in the west. It's studded with numerous islands of all sizes, the most famous of which is Miyajima, home of the Itsukushima Shrine. Cruises ply the waters of the Seto Inland Sea, as do regular ferries sailing between Honshu, Shikoku, and Kyushu. The adventuresome can even cycle across the Seto Inland Sea via the Shimanami Kaido route linking Honshu with Shikoku

Unzen-Amakusa National Park: At western Kyushu's high-altitude national park, you can climb Mount Fugen (1,360m/4,462 ft. above sea level), relax in a hot-spring bath, and take a walk through the Hells, the park's extra-steamy sulfur springs.

Iriomote National Park: Japan's southernmost national park includes Iriomote Island, 80% of which is blanketed with subtropical forest and mangroves, as well as coral reefs and coastline. Part of the Okinawan island chain, it's a mecca for nature enthusiasts and scuba divers alike.

Towada-Hachimantai National Park: Tohoku's most popular park beckons with scenic lakes, rustic hot-spring spas, hiking, and skiing.

Shikotsu-Toya National Park: This 987-sq.-km (381-sq.-mile) park in eastern Hokkaido encompasses lakes, volcanoes, and famous hot-spring resorts such as Noboribetsu.

Daisetsuzan National Park: The largest of Japan's 28 national parks and some say Hokkaido's most beautiful Daisetsuzan boasts three volcanic chains, fir- and birch-covered hillsides, impressive Sounkyo Gorge, and plenty of skiing and hiking opportunities.

Akan National Park: Popular for hiking, skiing, canoeing, and fishing, Akan National Park in Hokkaido is characterized by dense forests of subarctic primeval trees and caldera lakes, the most famous of which are Kussharo, one of Japan's largest mountain lakes, and Mashu, considered one of Japan's least-spoiled lakes and one of the world's clearest.

Best Dining Bets

Experiencing a Kaiseki Feast: The ultimate in Japanese cuisine, *kaiseki* is a feast for the senses and spirit. Consisting of a variety of exquisitely prepared and arranged dishes, a kaiseki meal is a multicourse event to be savored slowly. Both the ingredients and the dishes they comprise are chosen with great care to complement the season. There are hundreds of exceptional kaiseki restaurants in Japan, from old-world traditional to sleek modern; a standout is Kagetsu in Nagasaki. Traditional *ryokan* also serve kaiseki.

Spending an Evening in a Robatayaki: Harking back to the olden days when Japanese cooked over an open fireplace, a *robatayaki* is a convivial place for a meal and drinks. One of the most famous is Inakaya in Tokyo, where diners sit at a counter; on the other side are two cooks, grills, and mountains of food. You'll love the drama of this place.

Dining on Western Food in Modern Settings: Japan has no lack of great Western food, and some of the best places to dine are its first-class hotels. The New York Grill, on the 52nd floor of the Park Hyatt in Tokyo, epitomizes the best of the West with its sophisticated setting, great views, great food, and great jazz.

Buying Prepared Meals at a Department Store: The basement floors of department stores are almost always devoted to foodstuffs, including takeout foods. Shopping for your meal is a fun experience: Hawkers yell their wares, samples are set out for you to nibble, and you can choose anything from tempura and sushi to boxed meals.

Slurping Noodles in a Noodle Shop: You're supposed to slurp when eating Japanese noodles, which are prepared in almost as many different ways as there are regions. Noodle shops range from stand-up counters to traditional restaurants; one of my favorites is Raitei in Kamakura.

Rubbing Elbows in a Izakaya: Izakaya are pubs in Japan usually tiny affairs with just a counter, serving up skewered grilled chicken, fish, and other fare. They're good places to meet the natives and are inexpensive as well. You'll find them in every nightlife district in the country.

The Best Outdoor Pursuits

Climbing Mount Fuji: Okay, so climbing Japan's tallest 3,766m-high (12,355 ft.) and most famous mountain is not the solitary, athletic pursuit you may have envisioned but with 400,000 people climbing it annually, it's a great, culturally enriching group activity. Many opt to climb through the night with a flashlight and then cheer the sunrise from the top of the mountain.

Hiking the Old Nakasendo Highway: Back in the days of the shogun, feudal lords were required to return to Edo (now Tokyo) every other year, traveling designated highways. Nakasendo was one of these highways, and an 8km (5-mile) stretch through a valley still exists between the old post towns of Magome and Tsumago. It's a beautiful walk, and the towns are historic relics.

Skiing in Honshu & Hokkaido: Host of two winter Olympics (in Sapporo in 1972 and Nagano in 1998) and riddled with mountain chains, Japan is a great destination for skiing, the most popular winter sport in the country, and for snowboarding. The Japan Alps in Central Honshu and the mountains of Tohoku and Hokkaido are popular destinations.

Cycling: Hard to believe, but you can bike between Shikoku island and Hiroshima Prefecture via the 70km (43-mile) Shimanami Kaido route, which actually comprises seven bridges and six islands in the Seto Inland Sea and follows a well-maintained, dedicated biking path. Another favorite: Cycling through the historic, rural Kibiji District in Okayama Prefecture on a path that takes you past paddies, ancient burial grounds, temples, and shrines.

Shooting the Kumagawa Rapids: You can glide down one of Japan's most rapid rivers in a long, traditional wooden boat, powered by men with poles.

Fishing: Most foreigners laugh when they see Japanese fishing spots a stocked pool in the middle of Tokyo or a cement-banked river, lined elbow to elbow with fishermen. For more sporting conditions, head to Lake Akan in Hokkaido's Akan National Park, where you can fish for rainbow trout or white spotted char.

Scuba Diving and Snorkeling: Okinawa, an archipelago of 160 subtropical islands, is blessed with coral reefs, schools of manta rays, and operators offering excursions for all levels, not to mention some of the best dive spots in the world. Favorites include the Kerama Islands and Iriomote.

The Best Temples & Shrines

Meiji Jingu Shrine (Tokyo): Tokyo's most venerable and refined Shinto shrine honors Emperor Meiji and his empress with simple yet dignified architecture surrounded by a dense forest. This is a great refuge in the heart of the city.

Sensoji Temple (Tokyo): The capital's oldest temple is also its liveliest. Throngs of visitors and stalls selling both traditional and kitschy items lend it a festival-like atmosphere. This is the most important temple to see in Tokyo.

Kotokuin Temple (Kamakura): This temple is home to the Great Buddha, Japan's second-largest bronze image, which was cast in the 13th century and sits outdoors against a magnificent wooded backdrop. The Buddha's face has a wonderful expression of contentment, serenity, and compassion.

Hase Kannon Temple (Kamakura): Although this temple is famous for its 9m-tall (30-ft.) Kannon of Mercy, the largest wooden image in Japan, it's most memorable for its thousands of small statues of Jizo, the guardian deity of children, donated by parents of miscarried, stillborn, or aborted children. It's a rather haunting vision.

Toshogu Shrine (Nikko): Dedicated to Japan's most powerful shogun, Tokugawa Ieyasu, this World Heritage Site is the nation's most elaborate and opulent shrine, made with 2.4 million sheets of gold leaf. It's set in a forest of cedar in a national park.

Kiyomizu Temple (Kyoto): One of Japan's best-known temples with a structure imitated by lesser temples around the country, Kiyomizu commands an exalted spot on a steep hill with a view over Kyoto. The pathway leading to the shrine is lined with pottery and souvenir shops, and the temple grounds have open-air pavilions, where you can drink beer or eat noodles. Don't neglect a visit to the smaller Jishu Shrine on its grounds it's dedicated to the god of love.

Sanjusangendo Hall (Kyoto): Japan's longest wooden building contains the spectacular sight of more than 1,000 life-size wood-carved statues, row upon row of the thousand-handed Kannon of Mercy.

Kinkakuji (Temple of the Golden Pavilion; Kyoto): Constructed in the 14th century as a shogun's retirement villa, this three-story pavilion shimmers in gold leaf and is topped with a bronze phoenix; it's a beautiful sight when the sun shines and the sky's blue.

Todaiji Temple (Nara): Japan's largest bronze Buddha sits in the largest wooden structure in the world, making it the top attraction in this former capital. While not as impressive as the Great Buddha's dramatic outdoor stage in Kamakura, the sheer size of Todaiji Temple and its Buddha make this a sight not to be missed if you're in the Kansai area.

Horyuji Temple (Nara): Despite the fact that Todaiji Temple with its Great Buddha gets all the glory, true seekers of Buddhist art and history head to the sacred grounds of Horyuji Temple with its treasures and ancient buildings.

Ise Grand Shrines (Ise): Although there's not much to see, these shrines are the most venerated Shinto shrines in all of Japan, and pilgrims have been flocking here for centuries. Amazingly, the Inner Shrine, which contains the Sacred Mirror, is razed and reconstructed on a new site every 20 years in accordance with strict rules governing purification in the Shinto religion. Follow the age-old route of former pilgrims after you visit the shrines, and stop for a meal in the nearby Okage Yokocho District.

Myoryuji Temple (Kanazawa): This is a temple of a different kind, popularly known as Ninja-dera and fun to visit because of its hidden stairways, trick doors, traps, secret chambers, and other Feudal-Era devices meant to thwart enemy intruders.

Itsukushima Shrine (Miyajima): The huge red *torii* (the traditional entry gate of a shrine), standing in the waters of the Seto Inland Sea, is one of the most photographed landmarks in Japan and signals the approach to this shrine. Built over the tidal flats on a gem of an island called Miyajima, it's considered one of Japan's most scenic spots. At night, the shrine is illuminated.

Kotohiragu Shrine (Kotohira, on Shikoku): One of Japan's oldest and most popular shrines beckons at the top of 785 granite steps on the Yashima Plateau with great views of the Seto Inland Sea, but for most Japanese, it's the "I made it!" that counts.

Dazaifu Tenmangu Shrine (Fukuoka): Established in 905 to deify the god of scholarship, this immensely popular shrine has a festive atmosphere and is popular with students wishing to pass school exams. The road leading to the shrine is lined with souvenir and craft shops; the Kyushu National Museum is an escalator ride away.

Best Hotel Bets

The Best Traditional Ryokan

Hiiragiya Ryokan (Kyoto; tel. 075/221-1136): If ever there was an example of the quintessential *ryokan,* Hiiragiya is it. Located in the heart of old Kyoto, it's the ultimate in *tatami* luxury: a dignified enclave of polished wood and rooms with antique furnishings overlooking private gardens. Six generations of the same family have provided impeccable service and hospitality here since 1861.

Tawaraya (Kyoto; tel. 075/211-5566): This venerable inn has been owned and operated by the same family since it opened in the first decade of the 1700s; it's now in its 11th generation of innkeepers. Located in old Kyoto, its guest list reads like a who's who of visitors to Japan, including Leonard Bernstein, the king of Sweden, Alfred Hitchcock, and Saul Bellow.

Ryokan Kurashiki (Kurashiki; tel. 086/422-0730): Located right beside the willow-lined canal of Kurashiki's famous historic district, this ryokan occupies an old mansion and three 250-year-old converted warehouses, yet it contains only five elegant suites, each with a tatami living room and sleeping quarters with Western-style beds.

Iwaso Ryokan (Miyajima; tel. 0829/44-2233): The setting here is as romantic as any you'll find in Japan. If you can afford it, stay in one of the ryokan's 80-year-old cottages, where you'll have a view of maples and a gurgling brook on one of Japan's most scenic and famous islands. If staying here doesn't make you feel like a samurai or a geisha, nothing will.

Hakusuikan Ryokan (Ibusuki; tel. 0993/22-3131): I'm usually partial to historic Japanese inns, but this sprawling complex right on the coast, with manicured lawns dotted by pine trees, offers an assortment of accommodations (the oldest building is 45 years old), along with one of the best hot-spring spas I've ever seen, modeled after a public bath of the Edo Era, as well as a museum filled with antiques.

The Best Western-Style Hotels

Park Hyatt Tokyo (tel. 800/233-1234 in the U.S. and Canada): Occupying the 39th to 52nd floors of a skyscraper designed by Tange Kenzo, this gorgeous property offers stunning views of the city, one of Tokyo's hottest restaurants, rooms you could live in, and legendary service. No wonder it was the hotel featured in *Lost in Translation*.

The Ritz-Carlton, Tokyo (tel. 800/241-3333 in the U.S.): Occupying the lofty reaches of Tokyo's tallest building, this luxury property in Tokyo Midtown ranks as one of Japan's best hotels, with Tokyo's largest rooms and coolest bathrooms (the two sinks and counters are at opposite ends, making them perfect for couples). It cocoons guests from the mad whirl of central Tokyo, yet Roppongi's hopping nightlife is just outside its doors.

Four Seasons Hotel Tokyo at Chinzan-So (tel. 800/819-5053): Surrounded by a lush, 7-hectare (17-acre) garden, this top-rated hotel is a wonderful respite in one of the world's most crowded cities, with its impeccable service and a terrific spa and health club.

Nikko Kanaya Hotel (Nikko; tel. 0288/54-0001): Dating from the 19th century, this rambling, old-fashioned hotel combines the rustic charm of a European country lodge with design elements of old Japan and it's just a 15-minute walk from Toshogu Shrine.

The Fujiya Hotel (Hakone; tel. 0460/82-2211): Established in 1878 and nestled on a wooded hillside, the Fujiya is one of Japan's oldest, grandest, and most majestic Western-style hotels. Resembling a *ryokan* from the outside, it boasts a comfortable interior of detailed woodwork, old-fashioned antiques-filled guest rooms, and a delightful 1930s dining hall. It also offers indoor/outdoor pools, extensive landscaping, and hot-spring baths. A stay here makes you feel like you've traveled not just to Hakone but to another century.

Shima Kanko Hotel Bay Suites (Ise-Shima; tel. 0599/43-2111): Its secluded setting on a hill overlooking a bay, hushed atmosphere, attentive service, and Zen-like decor make this 50-suite property seem more like a Japanese inn than a hotel. Enjoy the stunning views from the rooftop garden or from the privacy of your own bath or balcony.

The Westin Miyako (Kyoto; tel. 800/937-8461 in the U.S. and Canada): First built in 1890 but completely remodeled, this smartly appointed hotel sprawls across more than 6.4 hectares (16 acres) of hilltop on the eastern edge of town near many famous temples. Good views, a free shuttle service from the train station, indoor/outdoor swimming pools, and a Japanese garden make this a winner. There's even an annex with Japanese-style rooms as well.

Nara Hotel (Nara; tel. 0742/26-3300): From far away, this 1909 building just a short walk from Nara Park resembles a palace. Rooms in the main building have high ceilings, antique light fixtures, and old-fashioned decor.

Unzen Kanko Hotel (Unzen; tel. 0957/73-3263): This rustic mountain lodge of ivy-covered wood and stone was built in 1935 to cater to foreigners in search of Mount Unzen's cooler climate. It offers a casual and relaxed atmosphere, hot-spring baths, and comfortable, old-fashioned rooms not far from the Hells.

Towada Hotel (Lake Towada; tel. 0176/75-1122): This Japanese-temple-meets-Western-lodge property occupies a secluded wooded hill overlooking Lake Towada. Its oldest wing, built in 1938, was crafted by shrine and temple carpenters. It offers both Japanese- and Western-style rooms, all facing the lake.

The Best Affordable Japanese-Style Places to Stay

Homeikan (Tokyo; tel. 03/3811-1181): Although it's a bit far from Tokyo's main attractions, this is my top pick for an affordable, authentic Japanese inn in the capital. Rooms do not have private bathrooms, but pluses include a Japanese garden, nice public baths, and detailed *tatami* rooms adorned with traditional architectural features. Meals (optional) are served in your room. Another great plus: The owner speaks English.

Arai Ryokan (Shuzenji; tel. 0558/72-2007): Fifteen historic structures, all registered as national cultural assets and situated around a river-fed pond, comprise this sprawling *ryokan,* in business since 1872.

Ryokan Fujioto (Tsumago; tel. 0264/57-3009): This 100-year-old inn is nestled back from the main street of Tsumago, a delightful village on the Edo-Era Nakasendo Highway. Meals feature local specialties, and the father-daughter team running it speaks perfect English.

Antique Inn Sumiyoshi (Takayama; tel. 0577/32-0228): Located in the heart of Takayama on the banks of the Miyagawa River, this 90-year-old former silkworm factory features an *irori* (open-hearth fireplace) in the high-ceilinged communal room, antiques and painted screens throughout, and simple but delightfully old-fashioned tatami rooms overlooking the river.

Minshuku in Shirakawago's Ogimachi: Nestled in a narrow valley of the Japan Alps, Ogimachi is a small village of paddies, flowers, irrigation canals, and 200-year-old thatched farmhouses, about two dozen of which offer simple tatami accommodations and meals featuring local cuisine. This is a great, inexpensive escape.

Temple Accommodations on Mount Koya: If your vision of Japan includes temples, towering cypress trees, shaven-headed monks, and religious chanting at the crack of dawn, head for the religious sanctuary atop Mount Koya, where some 50 Buddhist temples offer tatami accommodations some with garden views and two vegetarian meals a day.

Miyajima Morinoyado (Miyajima; tel. 0829/44-0430): This public people's lodge, on picturesque Miyajima, is modern yet traditional and would easily cost four times as much if it were privately owned.

Tsuru-no-yu Onsen (Nyuto Onsen; tel. 0187/46-2139): This rustic inn, with a history stretching back to the Edo Period, thatched-roof building, and outdoor hot-spring baths, is as close as you can get to time travel. To really save money, opt for the self-cooking wing and prepare your own meals.

The Best of Modern Japan

Visiting Tsukiji Fish Market: One of the largest wholesale fish markets in the world, this indoor market bustles with activity from about 3am on as frozen tuna is unloaded from boats, auctions are held, and vendors sell octopus, fish, squid, and everything else from the sea that's edible to the city's restaurants. Be sure to bring your camera.

Attending a Baseball Game: After sumo, baseball is Japan's most popular spectator sport. Watching a game with a stadium full of avid fans can be quite fun and can shed new light on America's favorite pastime.

Seeing Tokyo from the TMG: On the 45th floor of the Tokyo Metropolitan Government Office (TMG), designed by well-known architect Tange Kenzo, an observatory offers a bird's-eye view of Shinjuku's cluster of skyscrapers, the never-ending metropolis, and, on fine winter days, Mount Fuji. Best of all, it's free.

Hanging Out in Harajuku: Nothing beats Sunday in Harajuku, where you can begin the day leisurely with brunch and then stroll the promenade of Omotesando Dori, shop the area's many boutiques, take in a museum and perhaps a flea market, and then relax over drinks at a sidewalk cafe and watch the never-ending parade of humanity.

Shopping for Japanese Designer Clothes: Japanese designer clothing is often outrageous, occasionally practical, but mostly just fun. Department stores and designer boutiques in Aoyama are the places to try on the styles if you have both the money and the figure for them.

Spending an Evening in an Entertainment District: A spin through one of Japan's famous nightlife districts, such as Shinjuku or Roppongi in Tokyo or Dotombori in Osaka, is a colorful way to rub elbows with the natives as you explore narrow streets with their whirls of neon, tiny hole-in-the-wall bars and restaurants, and all-night amusement spots.

Seeing Fish Eye-to-Eye in an Aquarium (Nagoya, Toba, Osaka, Kagoshima, Beppu, Okinawa): Because Japan is surrounded by sea, it's no surprise that it has more than its share of aquariums, many with innovative displays that put you eye-to-eye with the creatures of the deep. My favorite is the one in Osaka.

The Best Castles, Palaces & Historic Homes

Tamozawa Imperial Villa (Nikko): Comprised of a 1632 villa and an 1899 expansion, this 106-room villa was the home of a prince who later became emperor. You can learn about traditional Japanese architectural details and lifestyles of the aristocracy on self-guided tours, and unlike Japan's other imperial villas, it does not require a reservation.

Matsumoto Castle (Matsumoto): Popularly known as the Crow Castle due to its black color, this small castle boasts the oldest *donjon* (keep) in Japan (more than 400 years old). A moon-viewing room was added in 1635, and exhibited inside the castle is a superb collection of Japanese matchlocks and samurai armor dating from the mid-16th century through the Edo Period. Volunteer guides stand ready for personal tours.

Nijo Castle (Kyoto): One of the few castles built by the mighty Tokugawa shogunate as a residence rather than for defense, Nijo Castle is where the shogun stayed whenever he was in Kyoto. It's famous for its nightingale (creaking) floorboards that warned of enemy intruders. The castle is considered the quintessence of Momoyama architecture.

Kyoto Imperial Palace (Kyoto): Home to Japan's imperial family from the 14th to the 19th centuries, this palace is praised for its Heian design and graceful garden. Good news for travelers: Guided tours of the palace are free.

Katsura Imperial Villa (Kyoto): Built in the 1600s by a brother of the emperor, this villa and garden are considered to be among the best if not the best in traditional architecture and landscape gardening. More than anyplace else, the villa illustrates the life of refinement enjoyed by 17th-century nobility, when leisurely pursuits included such activities as moon viewing.

Himeji Castle (Himeji): Said to resemble a white heron poised in flight over the plains, this is quite simply Japan's most beautiful castle. With its extensive gates, moats, turrets, and maze of passageways, this UNESCO World Heritage Site has survived virtually intact since feudal times. If you see only one castle in Japan, make this the one.

Matsue Castle (Matsue): This 17th-century castle features a five-story donjon with samurai gear and artifacts belonging to the ruling Matsudaira clan, with many Edo-Era attractions just outside its moat.

Matsuyama Castle (Matsuyama): Occupying a hill above the city, this 400-year-old fortress boasts good views over Matsuyama from its three-story donjon as well as a collection of armor and swords of the Matsudaira clan.

Kumamoto Castle (Kumamoto): Although a ferroconcrete reconstruction not nearly as huge as the original, this massive castle is still an impressive sight, especially at night when it's illuminated. It's famous for its curved walls, which made invasion virtually impossible.

The interior houses a museum with palanquins, armor, swords, and other artifacts of the former ruling clans.

Shuri Castle (Okinawa Island): One of nine historic structures in Okinawa that collectively make up a World Heritage Site, this castle with Chinese and Japanese influences was the center of the Ryukyu Kingdom, which thrived for about 500 years

The Best Destinations for Serious Shoppers

For Everything: Japanese department stores are microcosms of practically everything Japan produces, from the food halls in the basement to the departments selling clothing, accessories, office supplies, souvenirs, pottery, household goods, and cameras, to rooftop garden centers. What's more, service is great and purchases are beautifully wrapped. You'll be spoiled for life.

For Designer Fashions: Tokyo's Shibuya District has the most designer boutiques in town, while Aoyama boasts main shops for all the big-name designers, including Issey Miyake and Comme des Garçons. Department stores also carry big-name designers; their annual summer sales are mob scenes.

For Souvenirs: Japanese are avid souvenir shoppers when they travel, so souvenirs are sold literally everywhere, even near shrines and temples. Nakamise Dori, a pedestrian lane leading to Tokyo's Sensoji Temple, is one of Japan's most colorful places to shop for paper umbrellas, toys, and other souvenirs. The two best places for one-stop memento shopping are the Oriental Bazaar in Tokyo and the Kyoto Handicraft Center, both of which offer several floors of everything from fans to woodblock prints.

For Traditional Crafts: Japan treasures its artisans so highly that it designates the best as National Living Treasures. Tokyo's Japan Traditional Craft Centeroffers a varied inventory of everything from knives and baskets to lacquerware, but there are many renowned shops in Kyoto and Kanazawa as well. Department stores also offer an excellent collection of traditional crafts.

For Antiques & Curios: Flea markets are great for browsing; you'll see everything from used kimono to Edo-Era teapots for sale. Japan's largest and one of its oldest monthly markets is held the 21st of each month at Toji Temple in Kyoto. (A lesser flea market is held there the first Sun of each month.) Tokyo also has great weekend markets.

For Electronics: Looking for that perfect digital camera, MP3 player, calculator, or rice cooker? Then join everyone else in the country by going to one of the nation's two largest electronics and electrical-appliance districts. In Tokyo, it's Akihabara, where open-fronted shops beckon up to 50,000 weekday shoppers with whirring fans, blaring radios, and sales pitches. In Osaka, head to Den Den Town.

For Local Specialties: Many prefecture capitals have a government-owned exhibition hall where local products are displayed for sale. Often called a *kanko bussankan,* the hall may have everything from locally produced pottery to folk toys and foodstuffs. Cities with kanko bussankan include Kanazawa, Okayama, Matsuyama, and Kumamoto.

For Porcelain & Pottery: Porcelain and pottery are produced seemingly everywhere in Japan. Some of the more famous centers include Nagoya, home to Noritake, Japan's largest chinaware company; Kanazawa, known for its Kutani pottery with its distinctive colorful glaze; Matsuyama, famous for its Tobe pottery (white porcelain with cobalt-blue designs); and Kagoshima, with its Satsuma pottery, which comes in white (used by the upper class in feudal Japan) and black (used by the common people).

The Best of Old Japan

Splurging on a Night in a Ryokan: If you can afford to, splurge on at least 1 night in one of the country's best *ryokan,* where the service is impeccable, the *kaiseki* meals are out of this world, and glorious views outside your *tatami* room are of miniature landscaped gardens. You'll be pampered in a manner befitting an emperor; many of the nation's oldest ryokan were indeed born to serve members of the imperial court and feudal lords as they traveled Japan's highways.

Attending a Sumo Match: There's nothing quite like watching two monstrous sumo wrestlers square off, bluff, and grapple as they attempt to throw each other on the ground or out of the ring. Matches are great cultural events, but even if you can't attend one, you can watch them on TV during one of six annual 15-day tournaments.

Strolling Through a Japanese Garden: Most of Japan's famous gardens are relics of the Edo Period, when the shogun, *daimyo* (feudal lords), imperial family, and even samurai and Buddhist priests developed private gardens for their own viewing pleasure. Each step in a strolling garden brings a new view to die for.

Attending a Traditional Tea Ceremony: Developed in the 16th century as a means to achieve inner harmony with nature, the highly ritualized ceremony is carried out in teahouses throughout the country, including those set in Japan's many parks and gardens. Several Tokyo hotels offer English-language instruction in the tea ceremony, but my favorite locale is Gyokusen-en in Kanazawa.

Getting a Shiatsu Massage: Shiatsu, or pressure-point massage, is available in virtually all first-class accommodations in Japan and at most moderately priced ones as well. After a hard day of work or sightseeing, nothing beats a relaxing massage in the privacy of your room.

Relaxing at a Hot-Spring Resort: No country in the world boasts more natural hot springs than Japan, which has 19,500 different springs. Hot-spring spas are found in virtually all regions of the country and feature everything from hot-sand baths to open-air baths..

Spending a Day in Asakusa (Tokyo): Asakusa is the best place to experience Tokyo's old downtown, with its popular Sensoji Temple, Nakamise shopping lane with crafts and kitsch, and casual traditional restaurants. As in days of yore, arrive by boat on the Sumida River.

Exploring Kyoto's Higashiyama-ku District: Kyoto's eastern sector is a lovely combination of wooded hills, temples, shrines, museums, shops, and traditional restaurants, making it one of the best neighborhoods in Japan for a stroll.

Watching Cormorant Fishing: Every night in summer, wooden boats gaily decorated with paper lanterns will take you out on rivers outside Nagoya for an up-close look at cormorant fishing. The birds, maneuvered by fishermen in traditional garb, have tight collars around their necks to prevent them from swallowing their catch. Drinking and dining on board contribute to the festive air.

Walking to Kobo Daishi's Mausoleum on Mount Koya: Ever since the 9th century, when Buddhist leader Kobo Daishi was laid to rest at Okunoin on Mount Koya, his faithful followers have followed him to their graves and now tomb after tomb lines a 1.5km (1-mile) pathway to Daishi's mausoleum. Cypress trees, moss-covered stone lanterns, and thousands upon thousands of tombs make this the most impressive graveyard stroll in Japan, especially at night.

The Best Gardens

Rikugien Garden (Tokyo): It's not as centrally located as Tokyo's other gardens, but Rikugien stands out not only for its quintessentially Japanese setting but also because its vistas are unmarred by surrounding skyscrapers. Created in 1702 and later donated to the city by the founder of Mitsubishi, it boasts a strolling path around a pond complete with islets, teahouses, and arched bridges.

Sankeien Garden (Yokohama): Historic villas, tea arbors, a farmhouse, a pagoda, and other authentic buildings, all set in a century-old landscaped garden with ponds and streams, make this one of the most interesting and picturesque gardens near the capital.

Ryoanji Temple (Kyoto): Japan's most famous Zen rock garden, laid out at the end of the 15th century, consists of moss-covered boulders and raked pebbles enclosed by an earthen wall. It is said that it's impossible to see all 15 rocks from any vantage point; see if you can. Come early in the morning for some peaceful meditation and to beat the crowds.

Katsura Imperial Villa (Kyoto): Designed by Japan's most famous gardener, Kobori Enshu, the garden surrounding this imperial villa is, in my view, Japan's most beautiful. A "strolling garden," its view changes with every step but is always complete, perfectly balanced, and in harmony. It's well worth the extra effort involved to see it.

Saihoji (Kyoto): Popularly known as the Moss Temple, Saihoji boasts Japan's most famous moss garden, with more than 100 varieties spread around a pond and giving off an iridescent glow. It's especially beautiful after a rainfall.

Kenrokuen Garden (Kanazawa): Considered by some to be Japan's grandest landscape garden (and rated one of the "three best"), Kenrokuen is also one of the largest. The garden took 150 years to complete and consists of ponds, streams, rocks, mounds, trees, grassy expanses, and footpaths. Best of all, no tall buildings detract from the views. After Katsura, this is my top choice.

Koko-en (Himeji): It isn't old (it was laid out in 1992), but this is a wonderful surprise package of nine small gardens, each one different but typical of gardens during the Edo Period, which lasted from 1603 to 1867. Upon seeing what can be accomplished with skill and money in little more than 18 years, some gardeners may turn green with envy.

Korakuen Garden (Okayama): Rated one of Japan's three most beautiful gardens, Korakuen was completed in 1700 and incorporates the surrounding hills and Okayama Castle into its design. It's definitely worth a visit if you're in the vicinity, though personally, I like Kenrokuen more.

Ritsurin Garden (Takamatsu): Dating from the 17th century, this former private retreat of the ruling Matsudaira clan is an exquisite strolling garden that incorporates Mount Shiun in its landscaping and boasts 1,400 pine trees and 350 cherry trees. Stop for tea in the Feudal-Era teahouse and contemplate the view at leisure.

Sengan-en (Kagoshima): Laid out more than 300 years ago by the Shimadzu clan, this summer retreat with a 25-room villa was known for its poem-composing parties, held beside a rivulet that still exists. After touring the garden and villa, be sure to visit the nearby museum with relics belonging to the Shimadzu family. This garden is one of my favorites.

www.ingramcontent.com/pod-product-compliance
Lightning Source LLC
Chambersburg PA
CBHW021054080526
44587CB00010B/242